101 SIMPLE WAYS
to show your
HUSBAND
you
LOVE
him

KATHI LIPP

**HARVEST HOUSE PUBLISHERS**
EUGENE, OREGON

*Cover by Harvest House Publishers, Inc.*

*Cover artwork © Becca Cahan*

Published in association with Books & Such Management, 52 Mission Circle, Suite 122, PMB 170, Santa Rosa, CA 95409-5370, www.booksandsuch.com.

**101 SIMPLE WAYS TO SHOW YOUR HUSBAND YOU LOVE HIM**

Copyright © 2016 by Kathi Lipp
Published by Harvest House Publishers
Eugene, Oregon 97408
www.harvesthousepublishers.com

Library of Congress Cataloging-in-Publication Data
Lipp, Kathi,
101 simple ways to show your husband you love him / Kathi Lipp.
    pages cm
ISBN 978-0-7369-5702-1 (pbk.)
ISBN 978-0-7369-5703-8 (eBook)
1. Marriage—Religious aspect—Christianity. I. Title. II. Title: One hundred one simple ways to show your husband you love him. III. Title: One hundred and one simple ways to show your husband you love him.
BV835.L529 2016
248.8'435—dc23
                                                                    2015025539

**Printed in the United States of America**

22  23  24  25  26  27  28  / GP-JC /  10  9  8  7  6  5  4

*To Chris and Vikki Francis*

*When you bought me that computer thirteen years ago,*
*you did more than invest in a piece of equipment—*
*you invested in me at a point when there was no proof*
*that your gamble was going to pay off.*
*I am forever grateful that you had the holy vision*
*to see something in me that I would have never seen in myself.*

*Thank you for your example of loving God, loving others, and*
*loving each other. You are life changers.*

## Acknowledgments

Great thanks go to Erin MacPherson, Cheri Gregory, Susy Flory, Renee Swope, Michele Cushatt, and Crystal Paine. So grateful to each and every one of you.

Thanks to Amanda and Shaun, Jeremy, Justen, and Kimberly. Love you more than is reasonable.

My team: Angela Bouma, Sherri Johnson, Brooke Martinez, and Kimber Hunter. You are faithful, inspiring, and a gift.

Rachelle Gardner—proud to call you agent.

Rod Morris—you make writing 80 percent less painful. In other words, you are a miracle.

Harvest House Publishers—I love that I get to call you home.

To our families: The Richersons, the Lipps, and the Dobsons. All my love.

To my friends at Church on the Hill in San Jose, California, and especially Scott and Kelli Simmerok. So grateful to call you home.

And finally to Roger. You are the reason for all of this. How do you pay someone for giving you your life back? I will just keep showing up and loving you every single day. Shut the door, baby.

# Contents

# Preparing to Show Your Husband You Love Him

Thank you for showing up for your husband.

I'm excited that there is a group of women who still want to say, "My marriage is important, and my husband is important." Which, it seems, is not very fashionable these days. In fact, as I was writing this book, husbands who talked to me about what was important to them were almost apologetic.

"I'm going to sound like a caveman, but I love it when my wife dresses up for me."

"Is it OK to say that I love it when my wife has dinner on the table when I get home?"

Yes, much of what these men told me sounded like it came straight out of a happy housewives manual from the fifties.

Dinner.

Looking nice.

Spending time together.

A clean house.

Yep—it sounded positively archaic.

Since when did society get to determine what makes a man happy? If having a roast in the slow cooker makes my man happy, who am I to tell him he's wrong? (I still like it when my man kills bugs for me. Does that make me a betrayer of my sex?)

What we've come to understand is that what makes a man feel loved hasn't changed much. What has changed is the role women play. We are no longer solely caretakers of the home—we work outside the home (or inside, as many of us work or run businesses from our kitchen table). We have dozens of responsibilities in addition to keeping our man satisfied and happy. So how does a real, true-to-life wife actually get it done?

We need to keep it simple.

I'm not telling you to do all 101 things described in this book at the same time. Even Wonder Woman had to get her cape cleaned every once in a while. But I am saying, try these out—and see what your husband responds to. You may figure out a whole new way to love your man.

OK, 101 ideas is a lot. And while I can get pretty creative when it comes to loving on my man, I have friends who are way more creative than I am. So I asked them to contribute their best ideas. I've included ideas from some of my buddies who have giant marriage books and websites, as well as from friends who just have great marriages. I know you'll be as encouraged as I was reading through all their ideas.

## Super Simple Scriptures

If you are looking to see real change in the heart of your marriage, the best thing you can do is pray for yourself and your man. So in various places throughout this book I have provided some of my favorite Scriptures to pray for your marriage. Now, I could give you lists and lists of Scriptures to hang on to as you pray for your man (and in a couple of cases I do), but for the most part, I pulled up my favorites. One that has stuck with me over the years as I pray for Roger is Hebrews 4:12: "For the word of God is alive and active. Sharper than any double-edged sword, it penetrates even to dividing soul and spirit, joints and marrow; it judges the thoughts and attitudes of the heart."

If we want the heart of our marriage to grow stronger, praying Scripture, in my opinion, is the best way to accomplish it.

## Super Simple Scripts

Sometimes the way to show your husband you love him isn't an action, it's a statement. So I've offered a few simple scripts of things to say that will encourage your husband by showing him real love and affirmation. So simple—but so easily overlooked in our day-to-day lives.

It's easy to think, *He should know this already!* But it's kind of like the joke about the couple that's been married for fifty years.

*Wife*: "Why is it that you never tell me you love me?"

*Husband*: "I said 'I love you' in our wedding vows. If something changes, I'll let you know."

We wives need to hear our husbands express their love for us more than once. We need to hear it often in order for it to sink in and really be believed. And so does your guy. So work some of the simple scripts I've suggested into your everyday conversation.

## You, Your Husband, and His Personality

Before introducing you to the 101 Simple Ways, I want to introduce you to a friend of mine. Her name is Cheri Gregory, and she and I wrote *The Cure for the Perfect Life* together. Cheri is a flat-out genius. (It's always good to have a few of those around to help you with projects, right?)

While the 101 ways are important, we have to realize that every man is unique. Some are going to get positively giddy over a plate of brownies, while for others, their dream come true is to be left alone for thirty minutes.

And a lot of that comes down to their personality.

And that is why Cheri is here to help us all.

I love when a book provides tools, and that's what we have here, my friends. Tools.

In the section that follows, Cheri provides you with a quiz to give you a peek into your husband's personality. Then, she provides a ton of amazing suggestions to help you love on your husband with *actions*, *gifts*, and *words* that are totally appropriate for your man and his personality type.

To me, this is the keys to the kingdom. This is the secret code that unlocks our husbands and their personalities. So even though you're eager to get started with those 101 Simple Ways, I encourage you to set aside some time to work through the following section. You just might be amazed at what you'll discover.

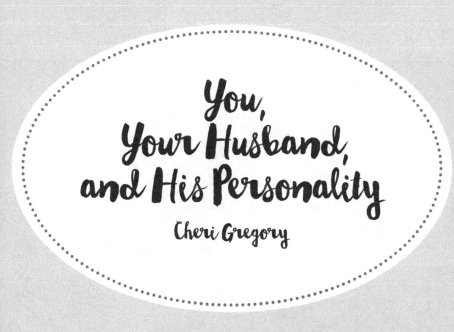

You,
Your Husband,
and His Personality

Cheri Gregory

# Assessing Your Husband's Personality Type

*The following questionnaire will help you determine your husband's personality type. For each scenario, circle the one response that you consider to be most true for your husband. If two are equally true, circle them both.*

1. In childhood photos, my husband

    **E)** was typically smiling or clowning around.

    **AN)** was sitting up straight with a serious look on his face.

    **D)** had an "Are we done yet?" look that conveyed his desire to get back to his own plans.

    **AM)** slouched, leaned, laid all the way down, or hid behind someone or something.

2. When board games come out at a party, my husband

    **E)** enjoys being part of a group and having fun together.

    **AN)** follows and enforces the rules.

    **D)** plays to win.

    **AM)** prefers watching others play.

3. When there's a sudden change of plans, my husband

    **E)** tries to look on the bright side.

    **AN)** will be distressed because what he'd expected is not happening.

    **D)** reacts in frustration, even anger, to the loss of control.

    **AM)** patiently rolls with it—"It is what it is."

4. If my husband had a day of free time, he would want to

    E) do something fun with family or friends.

    AN) take care of much-needed repairs around the house.

    D) start or finish a project.

    AM) "chillax."

5. If my husband's flight were to be delayed by five hours, he would want to

    E) strike up conversations with all the interesting people hanging out in the airport with him.

    AN) catch up on his reading.

    D) make progress on a project via his laptop and cell phone.

    AM) find a quiet place to catch a nap.

6. If a stranger were to watch my husband for a week, he would conclude that he highly values

    E) playing.

    AN) organizing.

    D) working.

    AM) resting.

7. My husband learns best by

    E) talking, active discussion, debate.

    AN) seeing, visualization, diagrams.

    D) listening, repeating aloud, hearing audiobooks/videos/podcasts.

    AM) getting hands-on, making a model, demonstrating a process.

8. If my husband were to enter a competition and do poorly, the worst part of the entire experience for him would be

    E) letting others down; not giving them something to cheer about.

    AN) making mistakes; trying to figure out what he'd done wrong.

    D) not being number one.

    AM) all the stress of the entire experience.

9. When learning a new skill, the thing that upsets my husband the most is

    **E)** being criticized.

  **AN)** trying to follow illogical instructions.

    **D)** failing to progress rapidly.

  **AM)** too much complexity.

10. The worst part about being sick for my husband is

    **E)** being isolated from people.

  **AN)** the germs, messes, and medications.

    **D)** all the work that's not getting done.

  **AM)** not feeling well enough to actually enjoy the R & R he's getting.

11. Behind his back, people probably say that my husband is too

    **E)** talkative.

  **AN)** obsessive-compulsive.

    **D)** driven.

  **AM)** lazy.

12. In school, my husband's response to a group assignment was typically

    **E)** gladness that he could receive class credit for socializing.

  **AN)** resignation that he would be the one to make sure the finished product was good enough to turn in.

    **D)** determination to make sure everyone did their part rather than just getting a free ride on his efforts.

  **AM)** satisfaction that there were plenty of other people in the group to make sure it got done (and usually at least one of them was far more invested than he was).

13. My husband is likely to find it difficult to respect an authority figure who is

    **E)** critical.

  **AN)** late.

D) incompetent.

AM) insensitive.

14. **My husband's biggest time-management issue is**

E) optimism: he acts as if everything will magically work out (and, if not, who cares if he's a little late?).

AN) deciding a project is "done enough": he gets so caught up in little details that projects often remain unfinished.

D) energy management: he starts too many projects and tries to do them all simultaneously.

AM) breaking a large project into smaller steps: he focuses on the expected end result and gets so intimidated that he puts it off, often until it's far too late to actually do it at all, let alone well.

15. **An important contribution my husband makes to his friendships and to our family is demonstrating how to**

E) really enjoy life.

AN) care about quality.

D) get work done.

AM) live at peace.

16. **If our family were to plan a trip together, they would rely on my husband for _____ (but then...)**

E) spontaneous enthusiasm and tons of excitement (but then he might forget to pack half the necessaries).

AN) alphabetized checklists for packing (but then he might become stressed from double-checking all the pretravel details).

D) leadership in setting concrete goals for the trip: where to go, what to see, how long to stay (but then he might tire everyone else out with a demanding daily agenda).

AM) a calm and easygoing presence, with a bit of dry humor that breaks any tension (but then he might dig in his heels right at the worst possible moment).

17. My husband's walk can best be described as

E) swaggering.

AN) pacing.

D) striding.

AM) sauntering.

18. When checking in to a hotel, my husband

E) tells the person behind the counter all about why he's come to town and asks for her best restaurant recommendations.

AN) asks for a room that's away from traffic and noise.

D) prays for no line and quick service.

AM) hopes the bed is comfortable.

19. Of the following, the one my husband finds most distressing is

E) rejection.

AN) chaos.

D) powerlessness.

AM) disharmony.

20. When my husband's plans don't turn out the way he expected, he's likely to respond

E) with disappointment shortly followed by a better new plan.

AN) with hours or days of letdown and wondering, "Why does this always happen to me?"

D) by blaming whoever messed up his plan.

AM) by making fewer plans.

21. When developing a relationship with a new boss (or other authority figure), my husband

E) tries to get to know him as a person.

AN) analyzes his expectations and strives to meet them.

D) tests whether he is worthy of trust.

AM) tries not to attract any attention for the wrong reason.

22. When it comes to a major project or chore, my husband

    **E)** enlists help and makes it a team effort.

    **AN)** likes figuring out exactly what needs to be done and doing it all correctly.

    **D)** gets an adrenaline rush from accomplishment.

    **AM)** may well do anything but.

23. My husband's favorite clothes

    **E)** include Hawaiian print (or other flashy) shirts and ties.

    **AN)** are monochromatic and classic.

    **D)** make a distinct and intentional statement.

    **AM)** feature comfort above all else.

Now, add up the totals by writing down the number of times you circled each letter:

    **(E)** Expressive = \_\_\_\_\_

    **(AN)** Analytical = \_\_\_\_\_

    **(D)** Driving = \_\_\_\_\_

    **(AM)** Amiable = \_\_\_\_\_

The highest score correlates with your husband's dominant personality type, and the next highest score indicates his secondary type.

**An Expressive Man**

*An Expressive Man's Goal in Life:*

To have a good time

*What Love Looks Like to an Expressive Man:*

Attention

Affection

Approval

*An Expressive Man's God-Given Strengths:*

Talkative, storyteller        Life of the party

Good sense of humor
Memory for color
Emotional and demonstrative
Enthusiastic and expressive
Cheerful and bubbly

Curious
Good on stage
Wide-eyed and innocent
Sincere heart
Always a child

### An Expressive Man's Potential Weaknesses:

Compulsive talker
Exaggerates and elaborates
Dwells on trivia
Cannot remember names
Scares people off
Too happy for some people
Egotistical

Blusters and complains
Naive and gullible
Loud voice and laugh
Controlled by circumstances
Seems phony to some people
Never grows up

## An Analytic Man

### An Analytic Man's Goal in Life:

To achieve—and maintain—perfection

### What Love Looks Like to an Analytic Man:

Sensitivity
Support
Space

### An Analytic Man's God-Given Strengths:

Deep and thoughtful
Serious and purposeful
Genius-prone
Talented and creative
Artistic or musical
Philosophical and poetic

Appreciative of beauty
Sensitive to other people
Self-sacrificing
Conscientious
Idealistic

### An Analytic Man's Potential Weaknesses:

Remembers the negative
Moody and down

Enjoys being hurt
False humility

Off in another world
Low self-image
Selective hearing
Self-centered

Too introspective
Guilt feelings
Persecution complex
Tends to hypochondria

## A Driving Man

*A Driving Man's Goal in Life:*

To have control

*What Love Looks Like to a Driving Man:*

Achievement
Appreciation
Loyalty

*A Driving Man's God-Given Strengths:*

Born leader
Dynamic and active
Compulsive need for change
Must correct wrongs
Strong-willed and decisive
Not easily discouraged

Unemotional
Exudes confidence
Can run anything
Independent and
    self-sufficient

*A Driving Man's Potential Weaknesses:*

Bossy
Impatient
Quick-tempered
Cannot relax
Too impetuous
Enjoys controversy and
    arguments

Will not give up when losing
Comes on too strong
Inflexible
Not complimentary
Dislikes tears and emotions
Is unsympathetic

## An Amiable Man

*An Amiable Man's Goal in Life:*

To have peace (often at any cost)

*What Love Looks Like to an Amiable Man:*

Respect
Self-worth
Harmony

*An Amiable Man's God-Given Strengths:*

Low-key personality
Easygoing and relaxed
Calm, cool, and collected
Patient and well-balanced
Consistent life

Quiet but witty
Sympathetic and kind
Keeps emotions hidden
Happily reconciled to life
All-purpose person

*An Amiable Man's Potential Weaknesses:*

Unenthusiastic
Fearful and worried
Indecisive
Avoids responsibility
Stubborn

Selfish
Too shy and reticent
Too compromising
Self-righteous

## Typical Personality Combinations

Your husband probably has a dominant personality type and a secondary type. The typical combinations are:

Driving + Expressive
Driving + Analytic
Analytic + Amiable
Expressive + Amiable

Let's take a closer look at each combo.

### 1. Driving + Expressive = a man whose specialty is leading

Combine the life goals of these two personalities, and you have a man whose motto is "My way is the fun way!" He is an extrovert who loves people and productivity.

### 2. Driving + Analytic = a man whose specialty is working

This man's attitude says, "My way is the right way." He likes to get things done—and done right. He is very project-focused. He prefers to associate with like-minded people; those who don't share his values are draining, even frustrating.

### 3. Analytic + Amiable = a man whose specialty is thinking

"The right way is the reflective way" for this man. He is an introvert who needs downtime to process all that's been happening and to restore his depleted energy reserves.

### 4. Expressive + Amiable = a man whose specialty is serving

For this man, "conflict is no fun." He makes it his aim to figure out how we can all just get along. He cares about people as individuals and values being a good friend, coworker, and neighbor.

## Masks Men Wear

Because our society holds up the charismatic leader as "The Quintessential Man," many men whose natural personalities don't match this ideal wear a personality mask. That is, they unconsciously adopt some behaviors of a personality that is not naturally their own.

Many Amiables don a Driver mask and many Analytics put on an Expressive mask as they head out the door for work each day. They act like extroverts from nine-to-five. But when they return home, they are exhausted, utterly drained from spending so much time behaving as people they are not.

Wives who don't understand their husband's true personality style may feel gypped: "He's a go-getter at work, but I can't get him to go do anything here at home!" "Everyone at work says he's the life of the party; how come he's dead to the world with his family?"

When a man's job not only fails to meet his personality needs but actually violates them, home needs to be his haven: the one place where he feels safe to be himself.

# How to Love Your
# Husband with Actions

Now that you have a better understanding of your husband's personality, here are some suggestions to help you love on your man with *actions* that are appropriate for him.

## Actions That Say "I Love You!" to Your Expressive Man

### 1. Laughing with him

Borrow DVDs of comedians, relax on the couch, and chuckle along. Our family loves Ken Kington, Michael Junior, Taylor Mason, and Ken Davis. We've watched them dozens of times, and they're funnier each time!

Read comic books together. When Daniel and I were expecting our first child, we devoured books from the comic strip *For Better or For Worse*. As the kids moved through toddler and elementary years, we followed *Calvin and Hobbes* faithfully. Once they hit their teens, we became *Zits* devotees.

For years, Daniel and I had a weekly ritual of listening to *Car Talk* and howling together at the outrageous antics of Click and Clack, the Tappet brothers. Now, we enjoy listening and relistening to their CDs while we're on road trips.

What other ways can you think of to tickle your Expressive's funny bone?

### 2. Laughing at him

Audience laughter is a powerful opiate for an Expressive. Inside each Expressive is a stand-up comedian dying to get out and find an audience, *any* audience. Laugh at your husband's humor, and you'll trigger his inner Sally Fields euphoria: "You like me! You like me! You really like me!"

There's pretty much nothing an Expressive won't do to get a laugh. And if you're not laughing, they'll crank it up a notch or two until you do. (And whatever you do, don't withhold laughter as a punishment for your Expressive man.)

*Caveat:* I'm *not* advocating mockery. If you don't know your Expressive man well enough to sense the difference between "laughing at" and mocking, skip this one until you do.

### 3. Inviting him on a "mystery trip."

The point of a mystery trip isn't the destination. The point is the excitement of being invited on a spontaneous trip and the anticipation of the fun the two of you will have along the way.

Keep things cheap and easy. Near Christmas, you can fill a couple of thermoses with hot chocolate, hop in the car, crank up the Christmas carols, and drive down Christmas Tree Lane together.

Any time of year, pack a sack supper and go to the mall, cameras in hand, for some "photo-shopping" together. Go on a picnic. Miniature golf. Do some local sightseeing you've always meant, but never made time, to do.

One warning: non-Expressive gals need to remember that perfection and achievement are *not* the goals of a mystery trip. *Having fun together* is the sole goal. If something goes wrong, relax and roll with it. No parking spots? Venting your frustration will spoil the fun. Practice ahead of time saying, "This just means I get to spend more time with you!"

### 4. Doing a chore together.

Most couples settle into a predictable routine of his chores and her chores. Just for fun, join your man in one of his chores, preferably one you know is low on his favorite list.

Expressives dislike isolation. When you partner with your Expressive man on a chore, you'll turn boring into a blessing.

### 5. Listening... for as long as he wants to talk

An Expressive man's ability to talk can seem relentless. He will keep talking until he feels heard. And he won't feel *really* heard until he has not just your ears but your eyes too.

You may be tempted to think, *All that chattering is just childish!* But the truth is, Expressives *never* outgrow the need to be heard.

He *will* keep talking. He *will* follow you wherever you go. If you listen, he will *finally* finish. (And *then* he'll leave you alone.)

## Actions That Say "I Love You!" to Your Analytic Man

### 1. Organizing an area of disorder

Sometimes, this has been as simple as putting my shoes away "where they belong" instead of leaving them strewn about for Daniel to trip over. Other times, it's been as daunting as gutting the garage.

When "where they belong" (whatever "they" might be at the moment) hasn't been well-established, I've researched solutions until we found one that works for both of us.

### 2. Showing up for important events

Daniel's gospel quartet practiced every Monday night for three hours in our home, fifty weeks a year for seven years. I'd heard every song they sang, multiple times...often the same short phrase over and over and over—"There's power in the...There's power in the...There's power in the..."—until I all but begged for *blood.* Just give me *blood!*

So I initially thought performances would be no big deal; I could just stay home with the kids rather than dragging them out to hear what we'd already heard over and over and...

Wrong. When I didn't show up, Daniel was crushed.

Conversely, when I spent a wedding anniversary tending the quartet's table at a local Market Night, I earned beaucoup big points with my man.

### 3. Giving him a room (or space) of his own

When we first moved into a four-bedroom house, I took over the spare bedroom and crammed it full of my sewing and crafting supplies, which I visited now and then.

One day, while at my brother and sister-in-law's home, I found Daniel sitting on the floor reading in Karen's lovely office. He looked up at me and said, in a voice of longing, "She has a room of her own!"

It took me two hours, once we got home that night, to shift all my stuff from storage in my craft room to storage in the garage, freeing up space for Daniel's office/music studio/man cave (complete with a door that opens, shuts, and—when necessary!—locks.)

### 4. Respecting his need for solitude and protecting his need for quiet

When we were first married, Daniel used to take off for a walk, a trip to a bookstore, even a backpacking trip without inviting me. It took me years to understand that his need for solitude was not a reflection of his commitment to me or his enjoyment of my company. As an introvert, he needs time alone, away from anyone who knows or needs him.

Now, I actively protect my husband's solitude by call screening, running interference when someone shows up unannounced on our doorstep, and even holding his cell phone for a few hours when I can tell that he's peopled out.

When Daniel decides it's nap time, I crate the dog (so she won't bark at stray air molecules), unplug the phones (and remove the batteries), and tape a "do not disturb" sign on the door. And then I remove myself so he's free to enjoy complete silence.

### 5. Planning ahead

For the Analytic man in my house, spontaneity means anything less than three weeks' notice.

His favorite surprise? *No* surprise.

So I keep an up-to-date calendar on the fridge. And whenever I add something to my schedule, I email him *and* leave a note on his desk.

This way, he never feels like I've left him in the dark, and he can always do one of his favorite things: plan ahead.

## Actions That Say "I Love You!" to Your Driving Man

### 1. Offering to take orders

This action is especially loving when your Driving husband is feeling overwhelmed. Tell him, "I have an hour during which I can do whatever you need me to do." Even if you just get one small task done, he'll feel more hopeful immediately.

If he's too overwhelmed to even know what he needs, invite him to think it over and let you know if something comes to mind.

### 2. Requesting his help

A Driver wants to feel useful. Necessary. Sure, you can get things done on your own. But seeking your Driver husband's help signals that you value the skills and expertise he has to offer.

### 3. Sticking to the bottom line

I used to regale my husband with the novel-length version of my day, every day. I ignored the glazed-over look in his eyes, determined that we were going to build a more intimate relationship via sheer volume of words.

In time, I shortened my end-of-day commentary to the blogpost version. Suddenly, I no longer had to chase him around the house to get his attention. He started voluntarily asking me, "So, how was your day?"

In the last couple of years, I've edited myself down to Facebook status update length. Amazingly enough, Daniel now asks insightful questions, wanting to hear more. He recently startled me by asking, "And how did you *feel* about that?"

But my greatest successes have been Twitter-sized comments, the carefully thought-out one-liners. This school year, Daniel has stopped what he was doing, looked at me in wonder, and said, "That was profound!" more than a dozen times.

Clearly, less really can be so much more.

### 4. Allowing for more than one "right"

When our house was being built, Daniel and I got into an argument over the spelling of our street name. He knew it was Toulum*ne* while I insisted it was Toulum*me*. I had practiced the spelling aloud hundreds of times, specifically so I would not get it wrong.

We finally drove to the development, simultaneously shouted, "*See!*" in triumph while pointing at different signs. Turns out, the city had goofed and spelled the street name one way on one sign, another way on the other sign.

Instead of going toe-to-toe with a Driver, consider that he may be looking at a different street sign, spelled a slightly different way. Allowing for more than one right allows for two winners and no loser.

### 5. Assuming positive intentions

A Driving man can get so task-oriented that he forgets about people.

When your Driver has "bull-in-the-china-shop" moments (or days), trust that the original plan involved only action, not collateral damage. As you discuss with him the damage resulting from his task-orientation, emphasize the goodwill you assume he intended.

## Actions That Say "I Love You!" to Your Amiable Man

### 1. Hanging out together

Just hang out. No plan. No agenda. No expectations.

Amiables love "doing nothing" with friends and family for extended periods of time. For non-Amiables, "doing nothing" is an oxymoron: if you're doing *nothing*, you're not actually *doing*.

Embrace the paradox. Doing nothing with an Amiable is a gift that gives back to the giver. You'll receive the gift of learning to be a human *being*—even for a little while—instead of such a human *doing*.

### 2. Creating a comfortable environment

When I saw Daniel beeline toward a hideous old chair at a rummage sale years ago, I knew I should have left him at home. My protests were futile; he loved the chair, and he was going to have the chair.

Over the next twenty years, he lounged in that behemoth daily. When it deteriorated beyond use, he mourned as if he'd lost a dear friend.

In a way, he had. He'd lost his soft place to fall at the end of each hard day. Realizing the importance of the comfort chair, I suggested a shopping trip, and we returned home with a new favorite chair.

You don't have to buy a new chair. Find what equals comfort and comfortability for your Amiable. Ideas:

| | |
|---|---|
| Comforters | Sweatshirts |
| Quilts | Oversized T-shirts |
| Blankets | Elastic waistband pants |
| Overstuffed pillows | Leggings |
| Beanbag chairs | Slippers |
| Fuzzy throw rugs | Moccasins |
| Cushiony couches | The World's Softest Socks |

Make them available and encourage their use.

When you show an Amiable that you understand his need for comfort, you signal that when needed, you'll be a safe soft place to fall too.

### 3. Accepting answers

For years, I just knew Daniel was holding out on me. I'd ask, "So, where do you want to go to dinner?" and he'd respond, "Whatever you want" or "I don't care." For the next hour, I'd badger him relentlessly, trying to pry out of him what he really wanted.

Since Amiables possess a will of iron, I never successfully cracked his encrypted communication. We'd end up at dinner with me silently fuming because I just knew he hated my choice but still refused to tell me what he really wanted.

Turns out, what he *really* wanted was for me to quit trying to decode nonexistent secret meanings and take him at his word. He really did...not...care.

So when you ask, "Where do you want to go for dinner?" and your Amiable man says, "I don't care," you can happily say, "OK, then let's go to Panera Bread."

Enjoy your soup and bagel...and trust that he's enjoying his.

### 4. Clearing the calendar

Although this applies to any time of the year, the holiday season especially brings myriad options for places to go, things to do, and people to see. Christmas concerts, Scrooge plays, Santa Claus Lane. Classic movies to watch, cookies to bake, gifts to wrap. Friends, family, work associates. None are likely bad choices—most are actually good or even excellent.

But for an Amiable, the best place to go is nowhere. The best thing to do is nothing. And the best people are beloved family members and friends who come to the house to visit.

Crammed calendar = a *dis*tressed Amiable.

Cleared calendar = a *de*stressed Amiable.

### 5. Encouraging kinesthetic and aesthetic expression

Do you know what your man used to be famous for?

In my twenty years of teaching, I've noticed that my Amiable students are often gifted in musical, artistic, and kinesthetic expression.

When your Amiable was younger, did he sing solos in the school choir or play first chair in the band? Paint, draw, or do amazing woodwork? Lead a sports team, run marathons, or lift weights?

Don't know? Do some detective work! If you have easy access, check out his high school yearbooks and family photo albums. Talk to his family and longtime friends.

If you do uncover a talent that he's put on the shelf, encourage him to dust it off. If he says he's too busy, ask him to do it just for you, and then be his admiring audience. Reconnecting with a key piece of himself will pay huge dividends for both of you.

# How to Love Your
# Husband with Gifts

As newlyweds, Daniel and I made a point to relax together on the couch each evening. While we caught up on each other's day, I'd rub his neck and he'd give me a foot massage.

One day about six months into our marriage, Daniel stopped mid-sentence, got a quizzical look on his face, and asked, "Do you prefer foot massages or neck rubs?"

"Neck rubs," I said. "Which do you prefer?"

"Foot massages."

Armed with new knowledge, I started giving him foot massages, and he started giving me neck rubs.

We were happier on two levels. As receivers, we were now getting what we most wanted. And as givers, we knew for certain that what we were giving was greatly valued.

Selecting gifts that match your husband's personality type can give this same mutual satisfaction. Gifts that connect with your husband's personality goals and emotional needs are likely to be received as highly practical. And on a deeper level, they demonstrate your understanding and respect of who he is as a person.

Here are some quick reminders and ideas to get you started.

### Expressive Personality

*Goal:* Fun

*Needs:* Attention and approval

*Gift ideas:*

- comedy DVDs to watch and laugh at together

- invitation for a "mystery trip" together
- a ridiculous gag gift

## Analytic Personality

*Goal*: Perfection
*Needs*: Sensitivity and order
*Gift ideas*:
- organizational device for some area of disorder in the house
- "Quiet Coupons" he can use when he needs silence and solitude
- a book that combines key interests (I keep an eye out for books on the brain and music, as Daniel is fascinated by both)

## Driver Personality

*Goal*: Control
*Needs*: Achievement and appreciation
*Gift ideas*:
- the latest does-it-all gadget
- an engraved pen and pencil set (for making and checking items off lists)
- a customized World's Best Husband award

## Amiable Personality

*Goal*: Peace
*Needs*: Self-Worth and respect
*Gift ideas*:
- a beanbag chair or comfortable blanket for chillaxing
- a CD of a favorite musician or genre of music
- an energy-saving device (clap-on/clap-off lights, remote finder)

## The One-Size-Fits-All Gift

Write, print, and frame a list of things you love about your man.

- If he's Expressive, be sure to include the ways he makes you smile and laugh.
- If he's Analytic, list how he makes your life better.
- For a Driver, focus on all he does for you.
- For an Amiable, note the ways he keeps you on an even keel.

What ideas would you add to these lists? As ideas come to mind, jot them down so you'll remember when gift-giving time rolls around again!

_____

_____

_____

_____

_____

_____

_____

# How to Love Your
# Husband with Words

In this chapter we'll look at some ideas to help you love your man with *words* that are appropriate for his personality. But first, a word of caution.

## How *Not* to Talk to Your Husband

Kudos to you for reading these words. Most readers probably skipped straight to the section on how *to* talk to your husband. Why bother reading about how *not* to talk to him? It's so much easier—and more effective—to jump straight to the good stuff, right?

Wrong.

What's easy is turning a deaf ear to how badly we can self-sabotage our own best attempts to love our husbands with words.

What's effective is identifying and breaking our bad verbal (and even nonverbal) habits before launching new ones. Otherwise, our bad habits will dilute—and pollute—even the most positive words of affirmation.

So we're going to start by looking at two negative communication patterns that undermine many marriages. Small changes in these two areas can make huge changes in how your husband hears and takes to heart your words of love.

### Breaking "Baditude"

Attempting the Complaint-Free Challenge was an eye-opener for me. Switching a wristband every time I complained, criticized, gossiped, or used sarcasm made me aware of how often I was expressing "baditude" (about ten times more often than I thought!).

Plus, I discovered some unconscious baditude triggers that I had no clue were even happening. Most of my triggers weren't serious, just a bit bizarre. One, in particular, involved my husband.

Daniel's music studio is upstairs, and my office was in the kitchen at the time. I'd be sitting in the kitchen, doing just fine, no problems, no negativity. But as soon as I heard him start to come downstairs—just the sound of his foot on the top step—I'd get hit by a sudden urge: *must complain.* The easiest target was my laptop. So Daniel would get to the kitchen, and I'd be fussing about my computer.

Now, he always walked into a no-win situation. If he offered to help, I'd say, "How come you always try to fix me? Why can't you just listen to me?" If he didn't offer to fix my computer and just tried to listen, I'd be all, "Why aren't you fixing it? I told you I have a problem—I rely on you to fix things for me!"

When I realized this was a deeply ingrained (albeit unintentional) habit, I was horrified. *This is psychotic! Why am I doing this?* I wondered. And then, *How long have I been doing this? We're going on twenty-eight years of marriage. If I've been doing this for that long, why is he still here?*

I took the whole situation to God in prayer, seeking to understand why I'd developed such a rude routine. Here's what became clear to me: Daniel would spend three to four hours at a time working on music. When he finally came downstairs, I wanted to reconnect with him on an emotional level.

And I certainly was reconnecting with him "on an emotional level." Unfortunately, my knee-jerk habit was to take a "bad breath is better than no breath at all" approach and settle for negative emotion rather than intentionally aiming for positive emotional connections.

Armed with this understanding, I came up with a revolutionary new technique. The next time my husband came downstairs, I used a single word: "Hi!"

It worked like a charm. Daniel started coming downstairs a lot more often.

One day, I told him what I'd learned, and he filled in his side of the story. All along, he'd thought my baditude was his fault. He thought there was something about his presence that made me upset. So he'd hide out upstairs, not eating or drinking, until he was feeling pretty desperate. It wasn't even because he feared my negativity—he just didn't want me to feel bad because of him.

How sad is that?

Now I know this chapter is supposed to be about how to love your husband with words. But for some of us, the first step to loving our husband with words is to banish our baditude by

1. quitting complaint

2. kiboshing criticism

3. gagging gossip

4. silencing sarcasm

I know, I know—trust me, I know! None of these feels fun or exciting or brag-worthy. But those of us who use our words as weapons need to lay down our swords and allow our husbands time to drop their defenses.

Want to get ready to really love your husband with your words? Try taking the Complaint-Free Challenge for a week and see what the Holy Spirit teaches you.

### "How" Trumps "What"

What you say is important. But *how* you say it is mission critical.

Think of the different ways you could say this to a girlfriend: "You're wearing that?"

"*You're* wearing that?" implies that the outfit is fine, but the wearer should not be the one to wear it. "You're *wearing* that?" suggests that the wearer might be better off hanging the outfit up as curtains rather than wearing it as clothes. "You're wearing *that?*" makes it sound as if the wearer should turn around and head back inside the house to change into something more age-appropriate.

Now, let's bring this tone discussion closer to home. Try saying these phrases pleasantly, angrily, and sarcastically.

- I did it already.
- Not right now.
- If you insist.
- Whatever you want, dear.
- Excuse me—my mistake.

Depending on the tone and accompanying gestures (hands on hips, hair flip, eye roll), each of these simple sentences can be an underhanded dig at your husband and his masculinity. And yet when he reacts, how easy it is to insist, "All I did was assure him that I'd do whatever he wanted…"

So here's another practical way to get fully ready to really love your husband with your words: Record a morning and evening conversation with your husband every day for a week. When you play them back, listen to your tone and ask yourself:

- How did I say what I said?
- Did my tone match my words or undermine them?
- Would I use this same tone if I had guests over for dinner? Why or why not?

## How *to* Talk to Your Husband

If you skipped the opening section of this chapter because you wanted to cut to the chase, do yourself—and your husband—a huge favor: go back and start at the beginning. Yes, this section is full of *fabulous* ideas for speaking your husband's love language. But in order for your words of love to have their fullest impact, your marriage's ongoing dialogue needs to be free from the diluting—and even polluting—influences discussed earlier.

### Create a Personalized Love Lexicon

During a school board meeting years ago, Daniel and the chairman got into a disagreement that quickly escalated into a full-blown argument. The next day, Daniel was still scratching his head, trying to figure out how the discussion got out of hand so quickly. He was especially distraught because he'd heard that the board chairman felt that Daniel had been disrespectful.

"I looked him in the eye the entire time we were talking," he said. "I don't know what went wrong."

"Is the board chairman of your same cultural background?" I asked.

"I don't think so," Daniel responded. Then the epiphany: "He's from a culture in which respect is demonstrated by *averting* your eyes!"

One short phone call later, and all was resolved.

Just like the same gesture can have two completely different cultural meanings, a word can have one meaning to you and another meaning altogether to your husband. So start with the assumption that you don't know for sure, and make a personalized dictionary of what various words mean to your man.

You might classify each word as "positive" or "negative." And then indicate *how* good or *how* bad on a scale of 1 to 5.

For example, for me the word *stupid* is a negative 2. But for Daniel? Negative 5 for sure.

*Good*, as in "I had a good day," is a positive 1 to me but positive 4 for my man.

How are you going to fill your love lexicon with words to use toward your man? Start by listening to the words he uses when he criticizes and praises people, especially other men. Which words does he save for the harshest reprimands? For greatest affirmations?

Listen to the words and tones of voice he uses when speaking about himself.

Watch to see how he responds to what other people say to him and about him. Which jabs from a close friend or family member irritate or dishearten him the most? Which words of gratitude does he bask in?

Here are some words to get you started sleuthing:

| Words of Criticism | Words of Affirmation |
| --- | --- |
| stupid | intelligent |
| lazy | hardworking |
| arrogant | humble |

| | |
|---|---|
| dishonest | trustworthy |
| disloyal | loyal |
| insensitive | perceptive |

And some space to record your findings:

| **Words to Avoid** | **Words to Use** |
|---|---|
| _____ | _____ |
| _____ | _____ |
| _____ | _____ |
| _____ | _____ |
| _____ | _____ |

## Choose and Use Identity-Reinforcing Nouns

Sometimes we affirm our husbands with descriptive words:

- "You're so *funny!*"
- "Thank you for being so *concerned.*"
- "Wow—you're very *creative.*"

Other times, we focus on actions:

- "I appreciate the way you *lead* our family."
- "You *sing* well."
- "Thanks for *taking care of us* even though you were tired."

But here's a little-known secret of loving your husband with words: nouns are powerful tools for bestowing *identity*. Here are the same affirmations as nouns. Can you sense a difference?

| | |
|---|---|
| comedian | leader |
| protector | singer |
| artist | caretaker |

Now before you start fretting about relearning sixth-grade grammar, here's the good news: You don't need to figure out whether you're using adjectives or nouns (or dangling participles, for that matter) when you affirm your man. *Simply add a noun at the end.* Here's what it might sound like:

- "You're so funny! You are a total *comedian.*"
- "Thank you for being so concerned. I'm so glad I have you as my *protector.*"
- "Wow—you're very creative. You are an *artist.*"
- "I appreciate the way you lead our family. You are a true servant *leader.*"
- "You sing well. I love having a *singer* as a husband."
- "Thanks for taking care of us even though you were tired. I don't know what I'd do without you as my *caretaker.*"

Since you're making your love lexicon by studying which words your husband responds to most positively, you'll soon have a long list of strong identity-bestowing nouns to draw from as you affirm your man with words.

*One caution:* Nouns can become labels, and we know from personal experience how harmful labels can be. Be prayerful and humble as you select identity-bestowing nouns. You have the power to build your husband up and call him forth to be the man God created him to be. You also have the power to cut him down with just a hint of contempt. Use your words, especially identity-bestowing nouns, with great care and God-given grace.

## Specific Ways to Say "I Love You" to Each Personality

### Words That Say "I Love You" to an Expressive Husband

Your Expressive husband needs you to be his biggest cheerleader. He wants your attention. He longs to know that you approve of who he is and what he does. And he knows for sure only when you tell him.

It may be tempting to think, *Oh, he knows I think he did a great job on...* But what's running through his head is, *Does she like it? Does she like it?*

Notice how your Expressive responds to your praise. If it's with relief—"Really? You liked it?"—he's been waiting and worrying that you didn't like it.

Some Expressive-specific sentence starters include:

- "I'm so happy I married you because..."
- "You're the most wonderful man in the world for me because..."
- "I miss your..."
- "Tell the funny story about..."
- "I enjoyed watching you..."
- "You always know how to make me laugh, even when..."
- "Tell me more about..."
- _____
- _____
- _____

Test and refine these based on your husband's particular preferences and add to the list.

*Caution:* The Expressive is the most NTN personality: No Test Needed. In your face. Over the top. Force of nature. Larger than life. So it's easy to assume that it's OK to cleverly bring him down a notch or teasingly cut him down to size.

Yes, he'll laugh at put-downs disguised as jokes. They're a form of attention, after all. He will take bad breath over no breath at all, any day. He'll even join in, as self-deprecation is a form of humor; it's also a great cover for digs that go too deep.

But realizing the power of words, and choosing to leave hurtful ones unsaid, is a wonderful way to communicate love to your Expressive man. He's already been called "motormouth," "dummy," and "nuisance."

Take care *not* to add your voice to the echo of wounding words.

## Words That Say "I Love You" to an Analytic Husband

Your Analytic husband needs you to be the one who understands him best. He wants your sensitivity to what makes him tick. He longs to hear your words of support. Although he'll never ask you aloud, your Analytic wonders, *Do you notice? Do you see all the detailed work I'm putting in...for you?*

And while his response is likely to be very subdued, you will see just a glimmer of satisfaction in your Analytic man's eyes when he realizes your answer is, "Yes, I notice. Yes, I see *all* that you do. Yes, I realize it's for me."

Some Analytic-specific sentence starters include:

* "I can always count on you to..."
* "I'm confused about ____. Could you help me understand it better?"
* "How did you get the idea to...?"
* "I love how you never give up, even when..."
* "That was so smart of you to..."
* "You showed such integrity when..."
* "The details were fully covered when you..."
* _____
* _____
* _____

Test and refine these based on your husband's particular preferences and add to the list.

*Caution*: Don't try to cheer up your Analytic. When things go wrong, he is reminded that he has, once again, failed to achieve perfection. He may take this failure to heart and become very discouraged for a while.

Trying to cheer up a discouraged Analytic is like trying to nail Jell-O to the wall: lots of effort with no results. You'll end up frustrated that your attempts aren't appreciated, and your husband will become further discouraged because you clearly don't understand him or the gravity of the situation.

While it's tempting to just leave him alone (and if you ask, you may even find out that's what he needs at the moment), your staying alongside him *without* trying to fix him may speak love the loudest...without you saying anything at all.

### Words That Say "I Love You" to a Driver Husband

Your Driver husband needs your recognition for his achievements. He wants your appreciation for his efforts. He longs for you to be his most loyal and devoted fan.

Sometimes, a Driver will start unconsciously boasting about his latest accomplishments in hopes that his wife will take the hint and join in. This isn't necessarily arrogance; it's evidence of how badly he desires your accolades. Acknowledge your Driver man and watch him bask in knowing that he is a man whose wife is proud of her husband.

Some Driver-specific sentence starters include:

- "I appreciate the way you…"
- "I admire your…"
- "Your energy is contagious when you…"
- "I'm so proud of you for…"
- "You have such a sense of justice for…"
- "I love the take-charge attitude you had when…"
- "Life with you is never boring because…"

- _____

- _____

- _____

Test and refine these based on your husband's particular preferences and add to the list.

*Caution*: Some Driver wives tell themselves, *Oh, he already knows what a great job he did. He certainly doesn't need to hear it from me!*

Oh yes, he does. More than you can imagine. He doesn't actually need to hear about the great job he did; he needs to hear about the way his efforts impacted you, personally and specifically.

A Driver often keeps thank-you notes nearby. All he has to do is open one up and read the words, "I'm writing to say 'thank you' for..." and he's reenergized by the reminder that what he does makes a difference.

Jot down a few sentences detailing the difference your Driver man makes in your life. Deliver it via email, USPS, face-to-face over a mocha at Starbucks, or in front of a few friends.

## Words That Say "I Love You" to an Amiable Husband

Your Amiable husband needs to feel your respect. He wants to be worthy of your love. And he longs for a harmonious connection between the two of you.

Your Amiable is the most understated and easily overlooked of the four personalities. His unspoken question to you is "Am I enough?" And his greatest fear is that he's letting you down, disappointing you in some irreparable way.

One of the greatest gifts an Amiable's wife can give her man is simply her delight in being the one person who knows him best and loves him most. Simple as it may sound, it is more than enough because it affirms that yes, *he* is enough.

Some Amiable-specific sentence starters include:

- "You make me feel safe when you..."
- "I don't know what I'd do without you to...."
- "You help me relax by..."
- "I feel so comfortable with you because..."
- "How did you manage to stay so patient with...?"
- "You were so kind to _____ when..."
- "I love getting to do life with you because..."
- _____

- _____
- _____

Test and refine these based on your husband's particular preferences and add to the list.

*Caution:* Because the Amiable is the most balanced personality, he is often overlooked. The Expressive is Mr. Popularity; the Analytic is Mr. Perfection; the Driver is Mr. Productivity. But what's an Amiable's claim to fame? Exactly what does an Amiable *do* best?

Um...well...

Why is it so hard to come up with a quick answer? Because it's the wrong question. The Amiable's greatest contribution to his relationships is not what he *does*; it's who he *is*.

In a society that sings praises only for measurable accomplishments, your Amiable man needs you to reflect back to him the invaluable qualities you see in him and the inestimable contributions he makes to your life.

Only you can give your Amiable red-carpet moments that matter. A few words from you mean more than any public ceremony. After all, the only audience he cares about is you.

101 Simple Ways

# 1

## The Company You Keep

*Take a close look at the friends you surround yourself with. Do you need to change (maybe even eliminate) some of those relationships?*

My friend Kate showed up out of breath and about forty minutes late. "Sorry I'm running behind, guys! Gregg got home late from work."

She sat at our table on the restaurant patio with the mostly eaten plate of taquitos and mini tacos and caught the eye of the waitress to order her iced tea. She was ready to settle in for some serious girl talk.

"Didn't Gregg know that you had plans tonight?" Bev said. "I hope he apologized."

I sat there kind of stunned. As far as I knew, Gregg was a loving and considerate husband. A really good guy.

But Bev couldn't let it go. "This is what drives me crazy about Ben. He's always coming home late from work, not even thinking about me and how long I've been home with the kids. It makes me crazy."

Bev went on like this throughout the evening. Harping on Gregg and Ben and any other husband she could think of. Finally, Kate had had enough.

"Gregg had a big project at work and his boss asked him to stay behind. He called to ask if I would be OK if he ran late—and I told him of course. I'm sorry I was late, but this was important."

Sometimes the Bevs in our life are going through a crisis of their own. Their husband is not in a great spot, she's feeling unsupported, and marriage is hard. In those instances, be a friend and love her through it. I'm guessing she wants to hang out with you because she desperately needs some encouragement.

But husband bashing—hers, mine, or yours—is never OK. I have a few select friends that I've been known to ask to pray for my marriage, but these women are champions of my husband. They are the ones pointing out the good in Roger, looking at his side, and generally in for the win of my marriage. And I feel the same about them and their marriages.

If the Bev in your life is constantly pointing out the bad in your man (or hers), it may be time to move on from that relationship.

Here are some things to consider when looking at the people you surround yourself with:

- *Does she speak the truth?* If she exaggerates the misdeeds (real or imagined) of the man in her life, it may be time to lessen your time with her.

- *When speaking the truth, does she do it with love?* So maybe her husband really does do some not so great things, but we can either approach our relationships with love or judgment. We don't get to do both. Is she speaking the truth but not with love? It may be time to move on.

- *Does she love being stuck?* Some people just love being stuck in their bad situation. It doesn't matter how many suggestions you make or ideas you offer—they just want to be stuck. Get out now before they start to limit your thinking about your own marriage.

## 2

## Know Your Man

*Pay attention to what your husband says he likes.*

It can be so easy to fall into expectations of what your husband "should" like. If he's like most guys, he loves sports, barbecue, and action movies. But what if you're married to a chess playing vegan who loves foreign films?

Celebrate the man you have! Pay attention to what he says he wants and take him seriously. There's nothing worse than planning something for your man, thinking, *Any guy would love this!* But you're not married to "any guy"; you're married to your guy.

"My husband had a big birthday coming up, but he doesn't like gifts or celebrations. I decided that the thing he would like best is to have his grown children with him, so I secretly arranged for our daughter and her husband to come up from San Diego and my local son to take off of work and come for dinner. The travelers arrived about midnight Friday night and snuck into the house. He had no idea they were coming and was totally blown away. He says that weekend was the best gift he could have received."—Susan Bringard

Here are some ways to up your noticing skills:

- I have a file on Evernote on my phone labeled "Hubby." When he mentions a movie he'd like to see or a recipe he'd like to try, I make a note of it in my phone. The next time I want to surprise him, I just go to my "Hubby" file where I've collected all my intel.

- I have an Amazon alert for Roger's favorite fiction author, Terry Brooks. When Mr. Brooks comes out with a new book, I'm the first one to get notified—and to order the book for Roger.

- In another file on my phone, I have a list called "Orders." When I want to order Roger's favorite drink at Starbucks or his exact order at In-N-Out Burger, I know what it is.

# 3

# Give Him a Break

*Figure out a way to give your husband a break—
especially at an extremely busy time.*

Yes, I know that you work hard too. And yes, if I could come over and scrub your kitchen floors to give you a break, I would. And no, you can't do all your husband's work for him every week. Marriage is a partnership. And I'll just say it—my husband is better at doing dishes than I am.

But sometimes, we need to jump in on each other's chores. This is why Roger and I know what our "stress weeks" are going to be.

For him, it's:

- whatever week he's working on our taxes
- Easter/Good Friday week (He's a tech/program director at our church.)
- Christmas week (see above)
- big projects at work

For me, it's book deadlines.

If your husband has his own stress week coming up, how about taking something (or a lot of things) off his list? I love Jennifer's attitude:

"My hubby works at a church, so instead of having Saturday and Sunday off, he has Thursday and Friday off. He was feeling stressed, and I decided to get all the household chores done Wednesday night so he could come home and have two days off. He was so glad I did my work plus his. He was able to relax, and he was very grateful."— Jennifer Helmholz

Here are some ways to help your man:

- *Get some outside help.* Could you hire a kid to mow the lawn, suggest that you pay someone to do your taxes, or offer to take the car in for an oil change? Explain that while you appreciate all he does, you want to help lift the burden. I've learned from other friends' experiences, though, that unless you know he hates those tasks, ask first. You don't want to send a message that you don't think he's doing his job.

- *DIY.* What can you do yourself to help your husband. Could you take his turn in the carpool so he can still workout? Walk the dog after dinner so he can get some work done? What is it that you could do to make his life easier this week?

- *The reason you had kids.* So they could start taking over chores! I gave my kids breaks when they had big projects coming up— they for sure could do the same for Dad.

················································· 4 ·················································

## Give Him the Word

·····················································································································

*Express to your husband the secret language of respect.*

The old adage is "Women need love, men need respect." In this one regard, men have it easy. A few heartfelt "I love yous" throughout the day will suffice for most of us womenfolk. But we need to get a little more creative when it comes to letting our husbands know how much we respect them.

Shaunti Feldhahn, author of *For Women Only,* has researched the ways that husbands feel truly respected. She says, "While we women enjoy hearing our man tell us 'I love you' often to reassure us of his love, men are not affected by hearing us say, 'Honey, I respect you,' but they do love to hear things like 'I'm so proud of you' and 'I trust you.'"

Here are some ways to express the secret language of respect:

- *Tell him why you're proud of him.* One day, I was coming out of the house just after Roger had left for a walk with our dog, Jake. Roger was almost out of sight, but I saw him bend down to pick something off the ground. It was the wrapper to a candy bar. How many people would pick up trash off the other side of the street? I let him know that I'm proud of him for always being a stand-up guy—when people are watching, and especially when they aren't.

- *Tell him why you feel safe around him.* It's the little things—like locking the deadbolt at night, texting me to make sure my flight got in OK, and checking my tires to make sure I'm driving safe.

- *Tell him the ways that you feel taken care of.* Does he take out the garbage without being reminded (or reminded only once)? Does he call and ask if he can pick up anything at the store? Let him know all the ways you feel cared for.

- *Tell him what a great dad he is.* One of the best ways to show respect is to let him know that you know he is a great dad. Point out all the ways that he goes above and beyond in his parenting.

# 5

## Simply Show Up

*Do life together with your husband.*

So much of what our husband wants and needs is someone simply to do life with him. He wants a partner in life and in fun.

How could you take an active interest in what your husband loves? Look at the lengths my friend Arlene Pellicane, author of *31 Days to a Happy Husband,* went to in order to connect with her man.

"It may sound odd, but one way I can affirm my husband is to in-line skate with him. Before you write this off as an easy hobby, please note I am terrified of putting anything with wheels on my feet. I was the kid who dreaded going to the roller rink for birthday parties. My husband, James, on the other hand was the kid skating with a boom box on his shoulder, Michael Jackson tunes blaring.

"Sixteen years into our marriage and into our forties, James bought me my first in-line skates for Christmas. I had a choice. I could make him feel like he bought me a vacuum cleaner or I could smile—and learn how to skate with the rest of my family (the kids got blades too; it was a nefarious plot in James's master plan). My first time on blades, I fell so hard on my tailbone that I sobbed. The second time, my ten-year-old son coached me so James and I wouldn't kill each other. The third time, I honestly questioned why I should have to learn this (painful and scary and dreadful) sport. I lay in bed the night before picturing myself falling over and over. As I skated cautiously and slowly, arms extended ready to brace myself, I realized something. Something big.

"I could throw in the towel that day and declare myself unfit for in-line skating. Or I could make up my mind that it was something I *could* learn. I saw in my mind the happy memories I could make with James if I could become his skating buddy (not whiz, champion, or expert...but buddy). My angst melted and I relaxed. I certainly didn't get much better, but I wasn't dreading it anymore. Later in the day, James said, "It shows me how much you love me when you try to skate. Thank you." For James, it's a huge stress reliever to have fun skating. It means a lot to him if I show up too—just to be his buddy."

Here are some ways that you can show up for your husband:

- Ask him to teach you a game that he loves. It can be a video game, chess, or another board game that he loves.
- Is there a sport your man would love to share with you? Could you go to the park and learn how to throw a pass or walk the dog? (Yo-yoing is a sport, right?)
- If having your husband teach you this new skill could be marriage-testing, see if you could have one of your kids, a friend, or a coach help you out. What a great surprise for your man too!

- Is there a book your husband has read and loved? Grab his copy and give it a read—and then invite him out to coffee to discuss the finer points of surviving a zombie apocalypse.

# 6

## Super Simple Scripts

*Tell your husband "I love doing* _____ *with you."*

Just that one little sentence can mean the world to your man.
I love doing life with you.
I love doing this parenting thing with you.
I love doing errands with you.
I love doing lunch with you.
So small a sentence, but so packed with meaning.

As much as you love all his accomplishments, as much as you love how he provides for your family and how he leads your tribe, saying "I love doing _____ with you" says "I love who you are. To your very core. You are exactly who I need in my life, and just being with you makes me happy."

Think of how you could slip this phrase into your husband's day.

- By text.
- Over the phone.
- In front of the kids.
- In front of his mom.

# Buy the Shirt

*Make sure your husband knows your
support for what he loves.*

What sport or activity is your husband over the moon about? If he's a 49er's fan, make sure you've got your red and gold. A graduate of Georgia Tech? Grab your Bulldog gear.

My husband graduated from Purdue University—Go Boilermakers! (Really? Couldn't he have gone somewhere with a cool mascot? How am I supposed to show my Boilermaker Pride?) So I order the shirts for him and wear mine with pride.

Yes, my husband is proud of his school, but really, if he were to pick a team, it would be team Walt. He is a bit of a Disney freak. And it always makes him happy to see me in anything Mickey—because he knows that I'm wearing it for him.

Think of some ways that you can show your husband that you're on his team. Whether his team is the Green Bay Packers or *Star Wars*.

- Buy the shirt. Get a T-shirt of something your husband is a true fan of. He will love nothing more than to see his girl supporting what he loves.

- If you're not a T-shirt wearing girl, buy the shirt and wear it to bed—with nothing else.

- Make sure it's a women's fit shirt. You want to look hot to your husband in every way possible.

# Getting Your Rhythm

*Establish routines that belong only to the two of you.*

It's great to have date nights and some special couple events, but there is a level of comfort from having a routine that belongs only to the two of you.

From the time we got married and had three kids at home (thirteen, fourteen, and fifteen—have mercy), Roger and I always made it a point to have a date night where we could just stare into each other's eyes and not talk about our children. Date nights cannot be oversold.

But there is something about the simple routine of a couple that can bring such a sense of support and security that we are hard-pressed to find in the world. We sneak in times when we can—we have lunch together a couple times a week, dinner together most every night that I'm in town, and every morning and every evening we walk our puggle, Jake. Yes, it takes just one person to walk a dog, but some of our best conversations happen on the walk around the block.

Three ideas to lift the level of routine in your marriage:

- If your husband is the cook in the family, can you be his sous-chef? Those unstructured times of cutting and chopping can lead to a greater level of intimacy. Who knew that carrots held such power?

- Nighttime routines are not only for the under seven set. Is there a little bit of a ritual you could build into your night? My husband loves almost nothing more than to have lotion rubbed into his back, and it helps him to have a restful night's sleep. An uncranky husband in the morning? Yes, please!

- Every night, we have a little time together to clean up the kitchen, get the dishes started, and feed the herd (two cats and a dog). Doesn't sound super romantic, but it's nice to have a signal to our brains that the evening has started and it's time to take the focus off work and the world and turn inside to those we love.

# 9

# Laugh

*Put as many places as possible in your
day to laugh with your spouse.*

Laugh. Often. Here are just a few ways that we make sure that laughter is a high priority in our house:

## Watch Funny Movies

Here are just a few that we love:

| | |
|---|---|
| *Shrek* | *Guardians of the Galaxy* |
| *Clue* | *Anchorman: The Legend of Ron* |
| *Ghostbusters* | *Burgundy* |
| *Princess Bride* | *Bruce Almighty* |
| *Cool Runnings* | *Liar Liar* |
| *School of Rock* | *Men in Black* |

## Discover Comedians

We love the Crackle show *Comedians in Cars Getting Coffee* where Jerry Seinfeld interviews different comedians while in cars getting...well, coffee. Some of our other, almost clean, comedians that we love are:

| | |
|---|---|
| Jim Gaffigan | Tim Hawkins |
| Jerry Seinfeld | Michael Jr. |
| Brian Regan | Ken Davis |
| Debi Gutierrez | Bill Engvall |

## YouTube Videos

We are a family of YouTube sharers. We love nothing more than to find the best video we can and share it with the family.

# 10

## Appreciating His Provision

*Make sure that your husband knows how*
*much you appreciate the work he does.*

Let me guess. No one in your husband's company is throwing him a party for showing up for work. No one is saying, "Great job on that spreadsheet, Bill. You really are amazing." Nope, for most of our husbands, work is a means to an end. And that end? Is providing for his family.

If your husband loves his job, great! That is a total bonus and something to thank God for each and every day. But if he doesn't jump out of bed and run to the office ready to tackle the day's challenges, that's even more reason to make sure that he knows you are appreciative each and every day.

I've said hundreds of times over the years that men want to know they are providing for and protecting their families, and you, his wife, are the only one who can let him know that he's doing a good job.

"One of the major ways I see God's provision for our family is through my husband's dedication to his job, and Derek is encouraged when I point out how his efforts help meet our needs. We are a two-working-person marriage, both contributing full-time to our household. I get paid for a bit of my work; my husband gets paid for more of his hours, with most of our family budget coming from his paycheck.

"We live somewhat simply, no fancy cars and vacations, but standard of living is irrelevant here. What matters is my recognition and gratitude for my husband getting up every day and heading to work. So I seize opportunities to specifically thank him for working hard so our ordinary needs are met. After a hard day at work, I thank him for facing his job-related stress. When I bring in the groceries, I thank him for the food about to fill our fridge. It's a way of saying, 'I understand I'm benefitting in a real way from your efforts.'

"As the mom, I'm in a position to point this out to our kids so they see, appreciate, and encourage Derek in this area too. When I highlight to our daughters how Daddy has provided for us in front of him, I offer the words of encouragement his spirit soaks up. If my daughter thanks me for a purchase when we're out running errands, I reply, 'Thank Daddy too when we get home.' When I'm at the park with our girls while Derek's at work, I text my husband photos with the caption, 'Thanks for making this happen, Daddy!'

"I don't want to take our comforts or my husband's work ethic for granted, so a simple yet specific 'thank you' is easy for me to offer and shows him I notice how his provision impacts our family in practical ways."—Alexandra Kuykendall

Here are just a few ways to let your husband know how much you appreciate the work he does:

- *Create a culture of thanks.* Not only is it important for you to thank your husband for the provision he's making for your family, it's important for you to do so in front of others—your kids, his parents, your parents, his friends. Make sure the world knows how proud you are of him and all that he does.

- *Change your mind.* It is so easy to get trapped in the world of not enough—not enough money, not enough time, not enough. But one of the worst things we can do is communicate that message to our husbands, because if they feel like they are not making enough, then they often feel like they are not enough. Even when finances are a challenge, changing your mindset to one of abundance can go a long way toward peace—for you and your husband. Listing the things you are grateful for will give you a different perspective even when you struggle to make ends meet.

- *Get specific.* In the story above, Alexandra shares specific ways her husband's job provides for their family. From the groceries to thanking him for getting to be home with the kids part-time, Alex is specific in what she is grateful for.

# 11

## Raid the Pantry Privileges

*Keep a few of your hubby's favorite foods on hand.*

This is a great way to make him feel not only loved but cared for. There is just something about having a few snacks on hand that can make working on balancing your bank account or watching a movie together more than tolerable, but downright enjoyable.

Here are some ideas of how to stock up:

- *Get him one small treat.* Maybe he lives for chocolate peanut-butter cups, but doesn't want the temptation of having them around the house. Could you pick up one at the store for him to have a special treat? (And no, he doesn't need to split it in half with the kids—or you. You can buy your very own treat.)

- *Keep a few healthy handfuls around.* My husband would put salsa on his breakfast cereal if societal rules didn't prevent it. And salsa? Is a pretty healthy snack. (What you're eating it with? That can be the culprit.) So I keep plenty of his favorite salsa stocked up so that he can dip in whenever he wants. He also loves air-popped popcorn and frozen juice bars. These are all guilt-free snacks, but they still let him know I think he deserves a treat.

- *The secret stash.* I am not tempted by certain snacks (Sour Straws? Ugh), but I know my man loves them. So I will buy a big pack, hide it, and pull two or three out every once in a while to surprise him. He always gets a sweet smile on his face when he sits down at his desk and there's a small army of Gummi Bears staring up at him.

# 12

## Create a Time Budget

*Make sure that some of your prime
time is budgeted for your man.*

You know how much energy you have in a week. Make sure that some of your prime time is budgeted for your man.

I've been known to give my husband the leftovers when it comes to my time. I have a full week of work, a full week of kids, then throw in some serving at church, as well as a little friend time, and well, my husband gets the equivalent of Tuesday's tuna casserole served on Thursday night. Plus, after forcing myself to become a morning person (trust me, it is possible), I am pretty useless after 9:00 at night.

But I am determined that my man needs more than the leftover me—he needs at least some of the best I have to offer. So I've set aside Tuesday nights, Saturday mornings, and Sundays.

Tuesday, my hubby and I have a standing date night (since I travel quite a bit, it helped to have it on a non-weekend night.) We make it early enough that I'm still at my best, and I can be the girlfriend he wants to date instead of the parent who is wrestling with kid issues.

Most weekends, I'm home at least Sunday afternoon, so that's when we'll plan to go somewhere together—out to lunch, on a car trip, or even just to the bookstore. Something that is just for him and me, some time to focus on what he needs (quality time is one of his biggies). And half the time, I'm also home Saturday morning, so my plan then is to linger over my husband. Have a leisurely breakfast, stay in bed a little longer than normal, and just be with him.

Before, I've tried to stay up late to have focused time with him, but with my early hours, I was not at my best. (No one wants their dinner date yawning through the details of their day.) Now I want to, whenever possible, reserve my best for my man.

Here are some other ways to give your best time for your best man:

- *Pick an unconventional time.* We think of dates as having to be at night, but what about a once-a-week lunch date or maybe even breakfast? With so many people working unconventional schedules, you need to determine what is right for you and your family.

- *Kid swap.* How about swapping babysitting with another family? You take all the kids Tuesday evening, and your friends get the whole gang on Thursday. That way, you have one guaranteed date night a week.

- *Make a plan.* Sometimes you're just in that crazy time of life when it's all so overwhelming you can't seem to make room for each other. Take five minutes over dinner, with both of your calendars out, to make a plan and stick to it. Even if your plan is week to week, you are still carving out some time for each other—and that's a very good thing.

# 13

## Pick a Part—Any Part

*Pick a part of your husband's body
and compliment him on it.*

My husband has a cute tush. He really does. I love it in jeans—or not. But I realized I'd never let him in on that little secret. He would constantly compliment me on various aspects of my physique that he particularly appreciated, but it never occurred to me that he might need the same.

So now I try to be liberal with my admiration. Since he's been running, I like to put my hand on his thigh and say, "Someone's been working out." When he decides to shave (we live in Silicon Valley so the standards for facial hair are pretty relaxed around these parts), I like to rub his cheeks and remind him how absolutely kissable that face is.

And let me tell you, he eats it up. He loves when I lavish on him. He loves that I notice the best parts of him. Sure, he loves it when I compliment him on his brilliant mind or the way he is so gentle with kids, but there's something in a man that needs to hear from his woman that he does it for her in every way possible.

Here are a few other ways to let your man know that you find him desirable in the most primal way possible:

- *Be verbal.* It may feel weird at first to speak such things aloud. But to compliment your husband's eyes or chest will ring in his ear all day long.

- *Be touchy.* Run your fingers through his hair (or over his heart if hair is no longer a factor). Put your hand on his thigh and give him a little squeeze with a soft "Mmmmm..." in his ear.

- *Frame your favorite recent picture.* Yes, it's great to have some classic pics gracing your home, but have a recent photo of your husband framed and hang it someplace where you spend a lot of time to let him know you love looking at him—now and forever.

# 14

## Super Simple Scripture

*When your husband feels overwhelmed,*
*pray that he will not live in that state.*

When my husband is overwhelmed, whether it's by work, family obligations, finances, or more, this is my favorite verse to pray for him:

The LORD is my light and my salvation—
whom shall I fear?
The LORD is the stronghold of my life—
of whom shall I be afraid?
(Psalm 27:1)

I love this verse. It reminds us that whatever we are battling, it is not all up to us. The Lord is the "stronghold of my life" and of my husband's life.

Sometimes it just takes a little perspective and a lot of support for your husband to get out from under that overwhelmed feeling. Overwhelmed is OK for a moment. But it's not OK to stay there. Pray that your husband will not live in that state.

## 15

## Don't Keep It G-Rated

*Make sure that your sex life is anything
but an afterthought.*

"There are many great options on how to love your man well. But I've found that there's one option that pretty well trumps all the others. I'm sure you may be able to guess what I'm referring to. Yup, it's S-E-X.

"Truthfully, when you think about it, sex is kind of the whole reason God created marriage in the first place. It was His idea and He encourages you to do it often (hence the whole "be fruitful and multiply" bit in Scripture). Yet, many times, this gets shoved to the bottom of the list when things get stressful or life gets busy.

"Can I let you in on a little secret I've learned in my twelve years of marriage? Keeping your man sexually satisfied and learning to *love* making love can transform just about every other area of your life.

"Look for ways to keep the spark alive. Flirt with your spouse. Whisper sweet nothings. Think about what you used to do when you were newlyweds and bring some of that sizzle back into your marriage.

"Not only can sex become the glue that serves as a foundation for a strong marriage, it also makes marriage a lot more fun and exciting. Put forth the effort, make it a priority, and I bet pretty soon you'll be singing the praises of how sex makes such a difference in your marriage too!

"Need some encouragement and practical advice in this area? I highly recommend reading *Sheet Music, Red-Hot Monogamy*, and *Rekindling the Romance.*"—Crystal Paine

Here are some simple ways to keep this a priority:

- *Flirt extravagantly.* Enough said.
- *Make it a habit.* Put it on your calendar. That doesn't mean you can't have sex on a nonscheduled Tuesday, but the longer you wait in between times of making love, the harder it is for you to prepare yourself mentally. Get it on the calendar and tell yourself, "We are the kind of couple who has sex twice a week!"
- *Lead up to it.* You can actually get yourself in the mood by looking forward to sex. Schedule it in advance. This helps you mentally prepare and get excited about being with your man.

## 16

## Heads-Up

*Give your husband a heads-up about upcoming plans and events.*

I am the worst. "Oh, didn't I tell you my mom was coming to stay? For a week?"

Fortunately, my husband really, really likes my mom. But I know that my man always does much better with a little heads-up. If I can give him a little warning, a "Hey baby, just so you know..." it makes a world of difference in how he handles the situation.

Here are a few ways you may want to consider giving your husband a little tip-off:

- *Text him—right away.* I get busy, it's understandable. But if I let him know when I know about plans that are being made, it avoids the awkward conversation of "Oh, baby...did I forget to tell you...?"

- *Get on each other's calendars.* With Outlook or almost any other email program, you are able to send events to each other. I use this tool a lot as an argument-saving device.

- *Put it on the fridge.* When my kids were younger and we were responsible for getting everyone where they needed to go, I had a master calendar of where everyone needed to be when. I would highlight in blue any of the pickups or drop-offs that Roger committed to. He didn't always pay attention to the calendar, but at least he wasn't frustrated with me for not telling him.

## 17

# Super Simple Scripts 2

*Tell your kids about the amazing things your husband does.*

"Let me tell you why your dad is so amazing…" It's such a simple sentence, but it encourages three people at the same time. Pretty powerful if you ask me.

"Let me tell you why your dad is so amazing. We were at the store and the woman in front of us was four dollars short on her bill. She was deciding what to put back when your dad handed the cashier a five dollar bill and said, 'Plenty of people have helped me recently. I'm glad I get the opportunity to do it for someone else.'"

By recounting to your kids something your husband did, everyone wins:

- *Your husband wins.* Your husband gets to be noticed for something he probably didn't think twice about. But you are saying to him, "I notice that you are a great guy, even when you don't think I'm paying attention."

- *Your kids win.* When you speak love and respect about your husband in front of your kids, you are training your kids to treat him with love and respect (which is easy when they are six, trickier when they are sixteen).

- *You win.* Let's face it—in marriage some days are rougher than others. It's good to be reminded—even if it's by yourself—what a good guy you are married to.

## 18

## Know the Truth—Your Husband Is a Visual Guy

*Understand that your husband is visual and what you can do to support him.*

I know that you know that men are visual. And I know you know how defeating that can be for us women. Especially if, like me, you have no chance of competing with the visual stimuli competing for our husband's attention every time he leaves the house (and don't even get me started on being at the mall or turning on the TV).

But I know that we are not powerless in this war of real women versus almost every piece of advertising, every movie, every television show created in the past thirty years.

We need to be what my friend and speaker Emily Nelson calls "visually generous" with our men. Here are just a few ways to do that:

- *Use lingerie—liberally.* Make sure to find a brand that is comfortable so you can wear it more than every anniversary.

- *Invest in great underwear.* I recently pitched anything that looked like it could be confused with my husband's boxer briefs. No more cotton briefs with busted-out elastic. A little frill, a little lace. Still comfy, but certainly girly.

- *Change in front of him.* Make sure he regularly gets a peek. Your husband will thank you.

# 19

## Give Him Time to Think

*Give your husband time to mull the ideas
you are talking to him about.*

"Men address issues by first pulling away to process and think so they can better talk about them later," says Shaunti Feldhahn, author of *For Women Only*.

Toastmasters, an international organization to help people develop their public speaking skills, does an exercise at every meeting called Table Talk. Someone stands at the front of the room, asks a question, and then asks someone in the audience to stand up and answer the question.

This is my husband's nightmare. Now most people would hate this for the mere fact that most people hate public speaking. (It's the number one fear in the US. Number two? Death.) But my husband's reason for being more terrified of Table Talk than of a tarantula? "I can't give an answer just like that. I need a little time to consider the issue. Get back to me tomorrow. Or better yet, this weekend."

And many men are like this. They don't want to give an immediate answer and regret it later.

One of the best things we can do as wives is to give our man a little time to consider important decisions. While I, and many women, are verbal processors (I like to hear myself talking an issue through), most men need a little space. They need to think it out before they talk it out.

Just a few ways to respect your man's brain and show him you love him:

- *Talk early.* It's Sunday night, and in the hustle of getting everyone ready for school, you remember that you need to turn in the form for your son to be on the traveling team for soccer. You kept putting it off because of the money discussion that it would bring up. But now there is a time pressure and a money pressure. Next time, give yourself and your husband the gift of talking to him as soon as possible so you both have some time to think it through.

- *Give choices.* Come with a couple of ideas of your own— without expecting an answer right away. You could say something along the lines of, "Here are a couple of ways I've come up with that we could handle it. Of course, you may have a better idea. Why don't you think about it and we can discuss it in a couple of days."

- *Set up a time to talk.* If you need his full attention, or are concerned that this could be a stressful conversation, set up an appointment to discuss it.

······················· **20** ·······················

## Make Him Feel Like a Hero

*You have the ability to make your husband feel like a hero. Use your superpower for good.*

Sometimes a man's perspective is a wonderful thing. Here is my friend Chance with his take on how to make your man feel like the superhero he really longs to be.

"Deep inside the heart of the man you love lives a boy who used to wrap a towel around his neck and pretend he was Superman. Sure, in time he eventually abandoned his dreams to fly. But like the rest of us men, he never truly let go of the hope that he could save the day at a moment's notice. And sometimes...he needs to see that he can.

"Where's a hero supposed to find a damsel in distress these days? It's getting harder and harder, especially when we consider our wives.

"We get it. You've made it abundantly clear that you can handle yourself—along with us and the rest of the world—just fine. And that's one of the things we appreciate most about you. But every now and then, when we're quiet and still, we secretly wonder if you'd even falter without us, or if you'd just find a way to keep moving forward—like you always have, like you always do. And so we wonder, *Does she even need me?*

"Most of us men spend our lives chasing after something bigger than ourselves, a moment of glory, a way to leave a mark on the world—our purpose. In time, our family becomes that purpose, that reason why. You're directly tied to our purpose and therefore our self-worth. As we age, we care less and less about what the world thinks of us, but we care more and more about what you think of us.

"So if you want to show your husband you love him, make him feel like a hero.

"It's not that he needs you to make yourself smaller than you are. It's that, every now and then, he needs to feel bigger than he is. So ask for help. Invite him into your problem. Even though you can solve it on your own, let him fix it. Then tell him how awesome he is. He needs you to need him...like he showed up just in the nick of time and saved the day.

"Whether he lets on all the time or not, your husband fully understands that you're a lot closer to being Wonder Woman than he is to being Superman. But every now and then, make him feel like a hero. Let him dust off his cape and remember what it feels like to fly."—Chance Scoggins

Here are three ways to make your man feel like a hero:

- *Use hero talk.* Tell your kids how strong, smart, and just awesome your husband is. Say it in front of them—and him.

- *Let him loosen the pickle jar.* Yes, I can grab the rubber twisty thing to help loosen the lid, but I prefer to let my man take care of it—and me.

- *Believe he can fly.* Let him know that his dreams are important to you and that you believe in him. That is what our men are looking for.

# 21

## Assume the Best

*Whenever there is a disagreement,
argument, or misunderstanding, assume
the best until you know otherwise.*

Six months. Six months is how long it took for me to answer the question. You see, for six months, every time Roger left the house, he would yell up the stairs, "Shut the door!"

And for six months, I was irritated.

"Why is he always telling me to shut the door?" I wondered. "Doesn't he trust me to lock up the house when I leave? I'm a full-grown woman. I don't need to be reminded every day."

For six months, I was irritated at my husband every morning. Until one day I couldn't take it anymore. Roger yelled up the stairs, "Shut the door!" and I ran right downstairs and confronted him about it.

"Why! Why do you always yell at me to shut the door? I am an adult. I can take care of myself!"

Roger looked at me, total confusion on his face. "I've never told you to shut the door in my life!"

"Yes you do. Every. Single. Morning. When you leave the house."

Then a look of understanding registered on his face. "Kathi, I'm saying *je t'adore*. It's French for 'I adore you.'"

For six months, I had been assuming criticism where my husband had been expressing only love.

How often do we do that in our marriages? He says, "Wow, I really like your hair that way!" and our thought is, *Wait—you didn't like the way I had my hair for six years?*

Oh sisters. We get it so twisted. Let us all assume love until further notice. If something feels hurtful or hard, take a breath, and have a conversation about it later (usually after you've calmed down is best).

Here are three ways to assume love:

- *Take a beat.* It's so easy to jump to conclusions, especially when we're hurt, tired, and stressed. But each of us could save a lot of emotional energy if we would assume the best and discuss with our spouse what confused us about what they said. *Confused* is a great word. It assumes love, but it also expresses that love is not what was received through those words or actions.
- *Ask for clarification.* And don't wait six months. Use phrases like "This is what I heard," and "I assume that I misunderstood."
- *Clear it up sooner rather than later.* Don't wait six months. That is not marriage building.

## 22

# Husband's Choice: The Dinner Edition

*Every once in a while, ask your husband*
*what he'd like for dinner.*

Over a year ago, I was at my friend Michele's house, being spoiled. (We should all have a friend like that.) Not only do we sit and talk for hours on end, this woman is a whiz in the kitchen. She is one of the few people I know who can make healthy food totally addictive.

In between the gluten-free, sea-salt, chocolate chip cookies and homemade hummus, Michele made me the life-changing chicken salad.

You think that's too strong a term? I would call anything that I now cook at least once a week life-changing. And why do I cook it once a week? Because my husband loves it. And I make it out of leftovers from his other favorite meal, my easy roasted chicken recipe.

### The World's Easiest (and Best!) Whole Roasted Chicken

1 whole chicken—giblets removed, rinsed, and patted dry

6 garlic cloves cut in half
½ stick of butter
garlic salt and pepper

Preheat the oven to 425°. Put the chicken in a roasting pan breast-side up. Salt and pepper cavity, put garlic cloves in cavity. Slice butter into pats and place all over the top of the chicken. Sprinkle the top with garlic salt and pepper. Roast until chicken's internal temperature reaches 165°.

### *Michele Cushatt's Chicken Salad*

3 cups of leftover chicken, diced
1 large lemon
2 cups nonfat, plain Greek yogurt
2 T. honey (or to taste)
1 green apple, chopped
½ cup dried cranberries
¼ cup slivered almonds
3 green onions, diced

Squeeze the lemon over the chicken and stir. Add yogurt and honey. Stir. Toss in chopped tart apple, dried cranberries, toasted almonds, and green onions.

Serve with crackers or lettuce cups...or eat it with a spoon right outta the bowl.

Every once in a while, ask your husband what he'd like for dinner. And if he has a healthy favorite that is an easy-to-prepare weeknight meal, put it in your regular rotation.

- If he's the cook in the family, support him in other ways (get the groceries, be his prep cook).

- When he mentions how much he's enjoyed a meal, make a note of it to put on the calendar again.

- Stock up on ingredients that can pull his meal together. The ingredients for the roasted chicken and Michele's chicken salad are on my grocery list every single week.

## 23

# Super Simple Scripts 3

*Thank your man for specific things he does.*

"Thank you so much for _____."

When we can specifically thank our husband for the things that he does, it shows him that we respect him for who he is and what he does. Here are just a few examples of specific ways to thank your man.

- "Thank you so much for being so kind to my mom. It shows me how much you love me—and her."

- "Thank you for taking leftovers to work today. I know how much you love going out. I appreciate that you are helping us save money."

- "Thank you so much for always taking the garbage out. I know it seems like a small thing to some people, but it makes me feel cared for."

## 24

# Learn His Language

*Learn as much as you can about what your husband does at work.*

Kanban boards. Scrum meetings. Ruby on Rails.

No. These are not martial arts terms. These are all things that my husband uses in his job as a quality engineer. And I know what all of them mean. (Mostly.)

For a long time, when someone asked what my husband did, I would wave my hand in the air and say, "He's a techie."

That would be akin to him telling people, "My wife? She writes stuff."

I needed to up my game. So I started to really pay attention to what Roger was talking about. And when I didn't understand a term, I asked him to explain it. (I may have even googled some terms on the sly so I could keep up with the conversation.)

Now I know that he is a quality engineer, helping other engineers be more productive. And because I am friends with some of his coworkers on Facebook, I know that he is really good at his job.

Here are a few more ways you can speak your husband's work lingo with him:

- *Ask him questions.* Even in occupations that seem pretty straightforward (I think we all assume we know what a firefighter does), there are still parts of your husband's day you probably know nothing about. Ask him what are his favorite parts and what is the most challenging.

- *Show up.* Or not. Before my husband started telecommuting, I would pick him up for lunch from his office every once in a while. He loved to introduce me around to the people he was spending his time with. Now I just wave to them on the monitor as they video chat. For some husbands this isn't a great idea (there are just some guys that want to keep work and family separate), so be sensitive to what he needs.

- *Tell your kids what Dad does.* Make sure your kids know what he does and how to explain it to other people.

# 25

# How to Compliment Your Husband: A Beginner's Guide

*Learn what your husband's "compliment target zone"
is and how to use it to your husband's advantage.*

"Every wife knows to compliment her husband, right? Tell him nice things about himself, brag on him to others, let him overhear you discussing his great qualities. But somehow all that wasn't working. Every good intention, every strategy fell flat and wasn't getting the result I had hoped for—the building up of my husband. Was he the one man on this planet who didn't respond to compliments? Was I doing something wrong? Apparently every wife *but me* knew how to compliment her husband.

"Then I stumbled upon a key to giving my husband a life-enriching compliment, one that spoke to his heart, that affirmed him as the man God created him to be, and connected us at a deep level. One that let him know I understood him, that I appreciated the same character traits in him that he valued in himself. The more I listened to him, I discovered what spoke to his heart, and that became my 'compliment target zone.'

"My honey takes his role of father very seriously. It matters to him to be there for our girls, to support and protect them, to provide wisdom and encouragement. He wants to provide the love and care of a father to them now that they are adults, even as he did when they were young. When I validate those traits in him, when I comment on how blessed the girls are to have him as their daddy, he feels confident and capable, still valued in a role that gives great meaning to his life. It's validating. It's bonding. It's encouraging and affirming. It's the most meaningful compliment I can give him. Well, that and a round of applause after lovemaking."—Carol Boley

You want to make your husband feel special by complimenting

him. Sometimes we have to be resourceful. Here are some ideas that might help.

- Find out what your husband's love language is. If words of affirmation are not what fills his love bucket, then all the compliments in the world won't make a big difference. Perhaps there is another way to make him feel encouraged besides words. Consider acts of service, gifts, physical touch, and quality time.
- Listen to your husband, watch his actions. What matters to him? If he couldn't care less about clothes, complimenting him on his attire won't make a hill of beans bit of difference to him.
- Some men may be embarrassed if you brag about them in public. You might consider a note on the mirror or a text message.
- Sometimes just saying a prayer for your husband can make all the difference in his day.

## 26

## The Best Part of Waking Up

*Do something the night before to make
your husband's morning a little easier.*

Suddenly, my husband is a runner. From "I'll be running only when a bear is chasing me" to "I'm going running, see you in a little bit," my husband has gone from walk to jock in the past few months.

As I want to keep the man around for the next several decades (I've grown attached to him), I want to support him in any way that I can. And one of the ways I can do that is by setting him up for his morning run the night before. I make sure he has a clean pair of sweats set out for him, and the ingredients for a healthy breakfast waiting for him for after his shower.

With your schedule and his, it may not be possible for you to be around in the morning, but you can set him up for success the night before. Here are a few other ideas of things you can do to help your husband's morning go smoothly:

- Set up his coffee.
- Make sure he has his smoothie ingredients (and that they are somewhere easy to see in the fridge or freezer).
- Move his keys and computer bag to the front door.
- Pack him a lunch.
- Bake some breakfast bars that he can take to work throughout the week.
- Get cash from the ATM for him to take for lunch.
- If you run errands at night, take his car and get it filled up with gas.
- Make sure he has clean clothes (nothing says "I love you" like clean underwear).

## 27

# Enough

*Make sure that your husband knows every day and in every way that he is enough.*

My husband would give me anything I wanted if he were able. A bigger house, a newer car, a larger wardrobe, and trips around the world.

But truly, that is not how we roll. We live in a tiny house. My car is fifteen years old. All of the clothes I have in the world could fit into two large suitcases. We've never left North America. And I'm fine with that.

When we first got married, I admit, I used to talk about all the things we could do when we had more money. But now—they just aren't that important to me. In fact, I have a secret desire to see how long I can go without buying another car.

My house is tiny—and I love it that way. (And bonus? Less to clean!) I love having a minimal wardrobe. There is a lot less time spent figuring out what to wear since my choices are few. And yes, we are saving up for a Europe trip for my next big birthday. But we are saving and paying cash for it. In a former life, I would have been happy to put it on a credit card.

I might have been dissatisfied at some point with all this—but I am learning to live with plenty and I am learning to live with little. And I am grateful for everything we currently have. Not what we will have in the future, but what we have today.

And I make sure that my husband knows, without a doubt, that I am thankful to God, and to him, for everything we have.

- Thank your husband for going to work. Or if he's unemployed, for looking for work.

- Thank your husband that, through your partnership together, you have the home that you do.

- Thank your husband for all the ways that he is more than enough for you.

## 28

## The No Talking Zone

*Some men just need some quiet. Give your husband some verbal space for a few minutes each night.*

I come from a very verbal family. We are big talkers, big laughers, big everything-ers.

My husband—not so much. Ah, the joys of falling in love with a true introvert.

It used to make me crazy that when we would be on a road trip for hours and hours, I was the one having to carry on the conversation. I eventually realized that the only one the silence was bothering was me. Roger was perfectly OK with no thoughts being expressed for sixty-plus minutes at a time.

In my family, if you weren't speaking, you were mad. In my husband's world, not speaking meant...not speaking. He wasn't thinking about anything. He wasn't stewing about anything. He just wasn't talking.

And while my husband does like to be greeted when he gets home with a "How was your day?" and more, I know that he always appreciates a little quiet time to just be by himself and recover from the day.

Here are a few other ways that you can incorporate "quiet time" into your man's day:

- *Have a "No Talking Zone."* Is there a location in your house where your husband just needs space? Ask the kids to give him a little verbal breathing room when he's in his study, in the garage tinkering, or in the bathroom.

- *Have a "No Talking Time."* If your man needs a little verbal break, how about giving him the first fifteen minutes after he gets home to just decompress from his day?

- *Let him lead.* Now when we're together in the car, I let my husband lead the conversation. Yes, if I have a topic I want to discuss, he's all ears. But there are times when a man needs to just go to his "nothing box" ("What are you thinking about?" "Nothing.") and just be.

# Play His Favorite Game with Him

*Get out your husband's favorite game—yes,
even if it's* Madden NFL *and you couldn't care
less about football—and play it with him.*

Every man loves some good old-fashioned competition, and when he
gets to compete with you at something he can win, well, you had him
at "Let's play Xbox."

Here are some ideas of how to get in the game:

- *Pick up a new twist on an old favorite.* I recently spotted a card
  game called *Monopoly Deal* at Target. I picked it up, and when
  Roger got home from work, I made a bowl of popcorn and
  asked if he wanted to play. He loved it because it was similar
  to one of his favorite games from childhood—and I loved it
  because it didn't take me twelve hours to buy Park Place.

- *Compete in an ongoing tournament.* Remember that thing
  about guys liking competition? Well, they do. So challenge
  your husband to an ongoing battle of wits with his favorite game. My friend Sarah and her husband have an ongoing
  *Ticket to Ride* tournament at their house. Whenever they play,
  the winner gets to put a check mark on a chart on the fridge.
  First one to ten check marks wins a thirty minute backrub.

- *Take one for the team and lose.* Now I'm not telling you to pur-
  posefully lose at that game of HORSE your husband wants
  to play, but if you were to, say, miss that layup and let him
  reign as champion of the basketball court for the rest of the
  day, he may not only feel macho and adored, but also like he's
  amongst the most loved men in the world.

# Ask His Mother

*Connect with your mother-in-law and
make her feel loved and not just liked.*

Sometimes your mother-in-law does not know what her role has transitioned to once you are married. She may feel at times like you took her boy. This transition is most likely hard on both you and her.

Here are some ideas from blogger Becky Helwig on how to connect with your husband's mother:

- *Call her on the phone.* Who doesn't like talking on the phone? A call is a safe space if you grind your teeth each time your mother-in-law comes over. She most likely is retired and feeling a little lost in her role as mother-in-law.

- *Coffee.* If you live in the same city, invite her to meet you at your favorite café. If there is any tension, this is neutral ground. Also, you do not have to entertain her at the café all day.

- *Have her come over and show you how to make your husband's favorite dish.* This is a bonding experience. By you taking the initiative, this leaves the power in your corner. Try to include her as much as you need or want. Also, now that you know how his mother makes his favorite dish, there should be no complaining about "this isn't how Mom makes it."

# Pray Him Up—Send Him Out

*Before or as your husband goes to work, pray
for his day and how he will walk through it.*

Movies portray strong men going off to work, leading their team, collecting their spoils, and returning to their castle triumphantly.

And then there's real life.

Many men feel like they are one big mistake from losing their jobs, even when they love the work they do or enjoy the teams they are on.

In work situations, there is a concept called "The Peter Principle," which asserts that "managers rise to the level of their incompetence." Sadly, many men feel like they got to their level a long time ago, and if anyone figures it out, they're toast.

And maybe it's not all in their head. Roger is well-respected at his job. I've met many people he's worked with, and they are all pretty glowy about my man. But for about three years, he worked with two people, one man and one woman, who made his life pretty miserable. These two had formed kind of an "office marriage" and loved working alone, just the two of them. Problem was, they were assigned to work with Roger. They would complain to their boss (who fortunately was onto the situation and paid it no heed), leave Roger out of email communication, and then they did something that rivaled the maturity level of a third grader: they put a whiteboard in the middle of their pod with their two desks on one side, Roger's on the other.

So every day for three years, I was sending my man into, if not a hostile work environment, a downright mean one. He would come home frustrated and sullen. Even though his boss understood what was going on, it made it hard to get work done when he was left out of key decisions and meetings. Plus, it wears on you when you've got someone actively hating on you.

So I prayed. The first verse I chose was Proverbs 22:29:

Do you see someone skilled in their work?
They will serve before kings;
they will not serve before officials of low rank.

(And by the way, it felt good to call these people what they were: "officials of low rank." Vengeful people are small people. And then yes—I prayed for myself.)

I wanted Roger to work on what mattered, with people who mattered. And within three months of starting to pray specifically for a new position, Roger got it.

Prayer is powerful and effective my friends. What do you need to be praying specifically for your man?

- *Pray that he would enjoy his work.* "So I saw that there is nothing better for a person than to enjoy their work, because that is their lot. For who can bring them to see what will happen after them?" (Ecclesiastes 3:22).

- *Pray for the reason that he works.* "Do not work for food that spoils, but for food that endures to eternal life, which the Son of Man will give you. For on him God the Father has placed his seal of approval" (John 6:27).

- *Pray that he would prosper in his work.*

  You will eat the fruit of your labor;
  blessings and prosperity will be yours.
  (Psalm 128:2)

## 32

# Surprise!

*Make all the plans, hire a babysitter, and
take charge of your date night.*

Sometimes, you just have to take matters into your own hands.

Plan a surprise date with your man, whether it's a spur of the moment coffee date, or stealing away for a weekend, or something in between, such as ordering the tickets to a movie he wants to see (and putting $40 in an envelope for two small drinks and a popcorn to share). And for a little inspiration, look at what Angela Grundy did to really surprise her man:

"I just surprised my husband. I found overnight sitters for all the kids and booked a hotel without his knowledge. I then sent him a text message right before he left work on Friday that read, 'Meet me at the Marriott room 308!' I bought something pretty to wear as well. I made sure to let him know how much I appreciated what he does for our family."

Here are some additional ideas to surprise the man in your life:

- *Buy a ticket.* Go away for a weekend somewhere that Southwest flies. Watch for sales—sometimes tickets can be had for less than $79 each way! Won't he be surprised when he needs his driver's license for your date, and he won't even be driving.

- *Swap a sitter.* Have your friend take the kids overnight, and do the same for her at another time.

- *Leave a clue.* Have something delivered to his office with a clue. Get a giant cookie with frosting that reads: "Meet me in front of your office, 5:00. I'll be wearing a red rose." (You can even make the cookie and have a friend deliver it.)

# Learn How to Make His Drink

*Figure out exactly how to make your man's
coffee (or tea) so you can act as his personal
barista every time he needs a pick-me-up.*

The barista at Starbucks has nothing on you—not when you know
exactly how many sugars and splashes of cream your guy wants in his
perfect frothy concoction.

Here are some ideas of how to get frothing:

- *Get your tools.* Duplicating Roger's Starbucks order is simple: a
  grande nonfat peppermint mocha, 180 degrees, no whip. Or
  not. Turns out that buying peppermint syrup outside of the
  month of December takes some ingenuity. And heating milk
  to 180 degrees without a thermometer is downright impossible. So I've had to get a bit creative in making sure I have all
  the tools to make Roger's drink for him. I stocked up on
  peppermint syrup last Christmas, and I bought a handy cooking thermometer at Williams-Sonoma. Which means if Roger
  is feeling a little down, I can whip him up a pick-me-up in five
  minutes flat (without even having to leave the house).

- *Go a bit overboard.* So, that perfect peppermint mocha? Well,
  let's just say I have been known to add homemade whipped
  cream, little candy cane sprinkles, and even some white chocolate shavings from time to time.

- *Surprise him at the office.* Any guy can take a break from the
  office and head to the Starbucks drive-through. But only the
  most loved guys get a favorite drink hand-delivered right
  when they need it most.

## A Weekly Menu

*While some men live for little surprises, for many guys,*
*knowing what's for dinner is their greatest love language.*

"I don't remember what prompted my question, but I do remember being surprised by my husband's answer. One afternoon I asked J.J. what his ideal week would look like (other than adding more sex, of course!). J.J. paused and thought really hard. Then he got a big grin on his face.

"'Now I'm not saying you have to do this,' he said hesitantly. 'But I would love it if you wrote out a menu each week and posted it in the kitchen so I could look forward to what we're having for dinner every night. My mom used to do that, and I loved it!'

"I realized for the first time that my husband's love language is food. And like many things, this was a personal preference we did not have in common. Truth is, I'm not a gourmet girl. I'd rather clean our toilets than plan our meals. It's sad, really. Especially since all four of my brothers love to cook.

"However, I am pretty crazy about my husband, and I knew J.J.'s dream come true was definitely doable. It's not like we didn't eat at home. But dinner time often included me scrambling at five o'clock to figure out what I was going to cook, and what J.J. might need to pick up on the way home from work. But he had never complained. In all the years we'd been married, he had never criticized my mayhem or lack of menu-planning skills.

"That day, I decided one way I could I show my husband I really love him would be to make his dinner-dream come true.

"As often as possible, I plan time for us to sit down Sunday afternoon and plan our menu for the week. Then I write it on a porcelain plate that's displayed in our kitchen, so J.J. knows what's cookin' as he looks forward to dinner together each night."—Renee Swope

Set up a weekly menu. Make sure it's somewhere that he can see it. On the fridge works great.

- *Put up his weekly favorite.* If he loves tacos, then make Tuesday Taco Night. Or maybe he loves breakfast for dinner. Do that on Mondays or pizza every Friday night. Give him something to look forward to at least one day each week.

- *Allow him to have input—or not.* Ask him if he'd like to have a say about the weekly menu. Some guys would love to tell you what they want; others are happy just to show up and eat.

## 35

# The Gift of Clear Space

*For many men, an uncluttered space to rest their eyes is the best gift you can give them.*

"I could try to affirm my husband by saying, 'Honey, thank you for going to work so I can stay home with the kids.' However, my husband's love language is *acts of service* and *not* words of affirmation. How can I affirm him where he knows beyond a shadow of a doubt that he is loved and respected? I need to speak his love language. I want my husband to feel over-the-top blessed when he comes home from a busy day at work.

"I hear the garage door open. He is home. First thing he sees is a clean garage. Shoes are on the shoe rack and the washer and dryer are clutter free. The kitchen door opens, and he is greeted with a sticky-free floor. Paper piles that covered countertops five minutes prior have been moved behind the closed office door. Children's toys that were crunched under feet are returned to the playroom thirty seconds before. He smiles and goes outside to give our three girls hugs. This is his perfect welcome home from a busy day.

"Reality sets in and rarely is he greeted with this gem. We have three girls under six, and our goal is to have the perfect welcome home three days a week. Yes, it is stressful, but we strive to reach success by being clutter free. Less clutter and more love."—Paula Tobey

If your husband's love language is similar to Paula's, here are some ideas of how to clear the clutter:

- Ask your hubby to send you a text when he is on his way home and begin picking up the garage, entryway, or living area so when he comes in, he feels loved and respected.

- Make a game of clean up with the kids by having a contest to see who can pick up more things and put them away in three minutes. Reward them with a special privilege, such as three extra minutes of their favorite activity.

- Greet your loving man with a beverage at the door, showing him that not only were you ready for his arrival, but he can see your love through service with a special treat as soon as he arrives home after a long day.

## 36

### Be a Copycat

*Make some of your husband's favorite treats at home.*

My husband's love language is petite vanilla scones and a 180 fat-free peppermint mocha from Starbucks. Sadly, seven dollars for a treat is a little out of budget for more than a once-in-a-while special occasion.

So I did my research. I googled "petite vanilla scones recipe" and found this amazing recipe on *The Pioneer Woman* blog. And the results? Amazing. Better than Starbucks (if you can believe it). Check it out for yourself at http://thepioneerwoman.com/cooking/2010/04/petite-vanilla-bean-scones/.

Here are some other ideas when it comes to loving your man through copycat food:

- *Go to www.copykat.com.* This whole site is dedicated to re-inventing your favorite restaurant recipes in your kitchen. The Cheesecake Factory chicken marsala is spot on.

- *Pay attention when you go out to eat.* Is there a food he just can't get enough of? Make a note to yourself and then go back and search for a recipe to make it happen.

- *Have a friend who loves to cook?* If cooking isn't your jam, pay a friend to whip up those Red Lobster Cheddar Bay biscuits for you.

## 37

# The Things He Does Right

*Tell your man specifically what he's getting right in your relationship.*

There are times when your husband feels like he isn't getting anything right. People at work are crabby, your kids are crabby, and maybe, just maybe, you're not having the best day ever.

All of this is contributing to the feeling that he's gotten it all wrong and continues to, and the chances of actually getting it right in the future? Slim to none. So it may be time to pull out the list-making skills that most of us women have.

"OK, so my hubby was feeling super bad about himself and told me that he felt like a failure at work and at home. We had a small fight, and during our fight he said, 'I just feel like I don't do anything right!' I felt horrible about it, and so the next morning, I emailed him at work and wrote for the subject line 'Things you got right.' And then I listed at least twenty things he does right all the time. Some of them were big deals and some of them not. Here's a selection of the things I wrote:

- during our late-night hot-tub talks, we shared our hopes, dreams, thoughts, and fears

- you attended every prenatal appointment
- you tickle the girls and make us all laugh
- you surprise me with flowers for no reason
- you cook a wonderful meal
- you kindly teach me things and not make me feel stupid
- you spent every night in hospital knowing how scared I was
- you remind me all the time that you love me
- you call and remember your mum, dad, grandma, and brothers
- you ask me what my favorite part of the day was
- you encourage me to do things I really want to but you're not sure about
- you go shopping with me and find better clothes for me than I do

"It made such a huge impression on him. He said he teared up at work and saved it as an important email so it showed up every morning. Then he talked about it later. That small thing made a huge impact that day and for many days to come."—Sherri Smetana

Here are some ways to share your list with your hubby:

- Send him one statement a day about something he did right.
- Like Sherri, send him one giant list that he can refer to over and over again.
- Post the list on your fridge or inside the garage so he'll see it every day when he leaves and gets home from work.

# 38

## Taking Care of Yourself Physically

*Invest in how you feel, and watch your
husband reap the benefits.*

When we take care of ourselves first, we are better equipped to take care of those we love. I know it sounds selfish—take care of ourselves first—but really, we are the only ones we truly have control over. And if we keep pouring out and never get refilled, we really are just giving everyone else sloppy seconds.

When I asked some of my friends how they showed their husband love, I loved this response from Becky Butterfield: "I've made my husband's year! I finally found something that helped me get the weight off that I'd been blaming and shaming myself about for years. Because I feel better about myself, I feel better about our relationship. He's one happy camper!"

We hear all the time, "Happy wife, happy life." But so often, we look at that as if it's up to the husband to make the wife happy. But we can determine a large part of our own happiness by taking care of ourselves in several ways. Physically is just one aspect of that.

Please hear me—I'm not saying lose weight to make your husband happy. I'm saying, take great care of yourself and value who you are. Because when you feel great about yourself, it can't help but leak into your marriage.

A few ways to take care of yourself physically:

- *Move, every day.* No, I will never be a jock. But I now am in the daily habit of moving. Whether it's improving my distance walking/jogging/crawling or doing Daily Burn True Beginner, every day I'm moving. It's improved my mood, makes me feel better physically, and makes me feel more confident.

- *Eat what makes you feel great.* Treats are great, especially when you share them with your man. But what is even better is knowing that when you enjoy healthy treats, you are fueling your body and caring for yourself.

- *Indulge.* I've always thought that massages were for "real" housewives who had more time than responsibility. And a "skincare regimen" was for the supermodel crowd. Now I indulge in both of these—the skincare twice a day, the massages once a month (especially when I'm on book deadline and hunched over a computer). They are nonfat ways of treating myself, feeling great, and relaxing.

## 39

### Know the Truth— for You, Love Leads to Sex for Him, Sex Leads to Love

*Understanding the differences about how we approach sex can make a better sex life for everyone.*

"Seriously? You want sex now?"

We'd just had a conversation about how stressful both of our days had been. Kids not making wise choices, long-distance parents who had needs we couldn't meet, and work situations that were stressing us both out.

All I wanted was a hug, some sweet words, and something that wasn't on my diet. Roger had something else entirely in mind. Both of us wanting to get to the love part—just in two very different ways.

My husband wanted sex because in his mind—and in the mind of your husband—during sex and after is when he feels the most love, the most connected. I wanted to feel loved and connected. And that would lead to sex (if other conditions were optimal).

So knowing what I know now, I try my best to go the extra mile. We'll both get what we need, it's just that sometimes we need to go in husband order and sometimes in wife order.

# Journey Through the Past

*Take your husband for a walk down memory lane.*

"Take your husband back to happy times from his past. The best part is that the woman he loves will be with him.

"If people have had a happy childhood or past, they love to reminisce about the things they did as a child or the fun they had with friends. Imagine how much your husband will enjoy someone else planning a walk down memory lane for him.

"Here are some ideas of how you can give him a journey through the past:

- *Plan a trip to his hometown.* (Do this only if your spouse had a happy childhood!) If you no longer live in his hometown, plan a trip back and just walk around the neighborhood. Stroll past his previous home, stop by the playground where he used to spend his time, check out his elementary school. This walk back in time may help you learn new and interesting things about your spouse.

- *Purchase hometown or college memorabilia.* Buy him a sweatshirt or T-shirt from his hometown or college. Every time he wears it, he will think of his happy memories from the past.

- *Sign up for news updates.* Sign up for local news updates from his hometown. Some local news stations have this or you could use Google Alerts.

- *Plan a friend reunion.* This may take a little more work and time, but you could plan a reunion of his closest friends. I recently did this for my husband. It involved a short trip and then an evening out for dinner with his friends and their spouses, and then he spent a day with his friends catching up and playing golf."—Robin O'Neal Smith

## It Really Is the Thought That Counts

*Do something for your husband that
you would never do for yourself.*

One of the best things about being married is knowing all those little facts about your spouse that no one else knows. One fact about my
husband? He loves a good salad-bar experience. (I'm guessing you were
expecting something a little juicer.)

He is always pretty appreciative when I make dinner. But when I
take the time to pull out the kitchen mandoline and slice up fresh veg-
gies, remember to pick up some feta at the store, and boil and chop
some eggs? He feels extra loved and cared for. So I reserve a little section
of our fridge that is just for containers of sliced mushrooms, chopped
onions, green peppers, and more.

No, I probably would never go to all that trouble just for my own
salad, but now that I do it, I do have to admit I'm eating more—and
better—salads.

Here are some other ideas when it comes to loving your man his
way:

- *Fold his clothes the way he likes.* I'm a sock folder—he's a baller.
  I do it his way because I love him.

- *Take notice.* Roger mentioned that he loved the smell of our
  new kitchen cleaner—it smells just like oranges. So now that's
  the cleaner I buy every time.

- *Let him do it himself (especially when he's better at it).* Roger saw
  a video online on how to fold a fitted sheet, and he is now
  the master folder in our home. I bow to his expertise, and he
  makes sure that it's done "right."

# Super Simple Scripts 4

*Reaffirm your husband's ability to take care of you.*

Our husbands have two deep needs that are rarely spoken of:

1. The need to know that they are able to protect you as well as provide for you.

2. The need to hear that affirmation from you (since you are the only one on the planet who can let them know if they are doing a good job).

Several years ago, I was teaching a writing course at a conference center, and while trying to connect with the wireless router, inadvertently hit something that allowed others who were on the network to see the content of the files of my computer. Another presenter noticed the problem and came over and helped me correct the issue. Then he said something I'll never forget. "Tell your husband he should be taking better care of you than that. I'm surprised he let that happen."

I may have lost my mind, ever so slightly. How dare he suggest that my man didn't take good care of me? I hit the wrong button on my laptop and that is the conclusion this guy came to? Is it that men are so hard on themselves, so some of them are equally hard on other guys?

I suspect this was an indicator of an insecurity in this gentleman. But if his statement got me as upset as it did, imagine what it would have done to my husband.

Here are some simple ways you can tell your husband that you are feeling well taken care of:

- "Thanks for suggesting I go lie down. You take better care of me than I take care of myself sometimes."

- "I feel so grateful for this home. Thanks so much for working so hard for our family."

- "You got my oil changed? Thanks so much for taking care of me."

- "Thanks for offering to pick up dinner. You always know when I need a break."

- "I so appreciate you filling up my car with gas. It may seem little to you, but it's huge to me."

······················· **43** ·······························

## Make Him the Biggest Target in the Room

*Be kinder to your husband than to*
*anyone else you meet each day.*

As you are passing out kindnesses throughout the day, make sure your husband receives more than anyone else on your list.

You're at a party and your spouse is across the room. He makes eye contact with you, the kind of eye contact that pleads, "Help! Get me away from this guy."

You're talking to a group of friends. You don't want to be rude, but you know that your husband is dying on the other side of the room.

Go to your man. Make sure that you are being kinder and more supportive of him than anyone else in that room. (This is especially true if your husband is an introvert and really didn't want to come to a party in the first place.) Here are some practical ways to show him kindness in that situation:

- Go refill his soda.

- Ask him in advance what time would be a good time to leave (and then stick to it).

- Brag on him within his hearing.

# Watch a Boy Movie with Him

*Let movie night be all about his choices—
and no guilt tripping, begging, or pleading
for that new romcom that just released.*

Let him pick the movie and watch it with him in rapt attention, even if you'd rather be reading a novel. Or cleaning the toilets.

Here are some ideas of how to make your movie night rock:

- *Give him a bunch of choices that he will love.* A few weeks ago, Roger said he'd make popcorn while I scrolled through Netflix to find some movie options. When he got back, I showed him four (yes four) *Star Trek* movie options and told him to take his pick. Now, I confess that my mind was secretly screaming, "Anything but *Star Trek*!" But I smiled as he picked option 3, and then I snuggled in next to him and did my best to comprehend life in a galaxy far, far away. (And yes, I know that's from *Star Wars*. But you get the idea...)

- *Pick up a new recommendation.* If you're seeing a lot of buzz from the male crowd on Facebook about some new action-hero movie, drop by Red Box and pick it up and tell your hubby you heard it was good.

- *Plan a romantic date night.* Take the initiative and plan a romantic date night for him. (And, for the record, while a romantic date night for you may include tickets to the latest drama, a romantic date night for him means action-packed or sci-fi. And lots of popcorn.)

# The Intentional Giver

*Show your husband your love through
simple gifts that fit his personality type.*

"I am so happy to be married to my husband and I want to encourage and support him in every way possible. The only problem is that I don't always show my appreciation in ways that he receives well. The turning point in loving and affirming my husband better was having him take Gary Chapman's free *The 5 Love Languages* profile (www.5lovelanguages.com).

"I thought that telling my husband how much I appreciate who he is and the work that he does for us was very affirming for him. It turns out that words don't mean much at all, but gifts make my husband feel loved in a huge way. Armed with this information, I decided to create a 'Gifts for Hubby' category in our budget, and I try to buy him one little treat every week. Most of the time it is some exotic food that I would never think of trying but which he loves. I have also given him books, a gift card to the movie theater, and DVDs because he loves reading and watching movies.

"I still tell my husband that I love him and I thank him for his hard work for us, but now I *show* him as well. It may seem like an insignificant change, but it has transformed the way my husband views himself and has increased his confidence in who he is as well as improving our relationship. Many times as wives we focus on trying to make big changes in our marriage, but the smallest acts can truly make the biggest difference."—Kimberlee Stokes

- Search online for "Love Language Gifts" and you will get tons of ideas for things you can do.

- Create that line item in your budget so you don't have to feel guilty about the money you are spending.

- Plan out your gifts for a month. It's easier to get creative in one big spurt than to try to come up with something new every week.

# 46

## Cheese Please!

*Come up with some cheesy but fun*
*ways to love on your man.*

"Buy things like heart stickers and kissy lip stickers and place them in random spots for him to find. You can put them on his sandwich baggie for work, on a Post-it and stick it with a stack of papers or on a bill you know he's going to pay later that day, for a few examples. It's a small and quick way to say 'I love you.' Stock up on these items around Valentine's Day and use them throughout the year."—Jenifer Metzger

"I hid *Star Wars* themed love notes for him to find around the house and in his lunch bag every day in February. He thought that was better than just doing something on Valentine's Day."—Katie Mower

A few more cheesy ways to say I love you:

- Cut hearts out of construction paper and make a garland with one letter of his name on each heart.
- Put lipstick on and kiss his side of the mirror.
- Buy a stack of heart-shaped Post-it notes and leave a note on his coffeepot in the morning.

## Pray Him Up

*Use the Scriptures to guide your prayers
for your husband's relationships.*

I have two men in my life who are at two different ends of the friend scale.

First, there's my husband. Most of his friends are "couple friends." We like to hang out with his friends, but usually one couple at a time. As Roger likes to explain about being a true introvert, "It's not that we don't like other people. We love other people. But most of the time we are most comfortable with ourselves."

And then there's my brother. An event isn't happening if it's not happening with a group of people. He is a true extrovert.

And both these kinda guys need prayer for their relationships.

Here are some of my favorite verses to pray for my man, from the kind of example he wants to be, to the kind of friend he wants to be. I want to be the kind of wife who is praying for him and his extended family, his friends, his relationships at work, and his relationships at church.

> Therefore encourage one another and build each other up, just as in fact you are doing (1 Thessalonians 5:11).

> If I speak in the tongues of men or of angels, but do not have love, I am only a resounding gong or a clanging cymbal (1 Corinthians 13:1).

> For by the grace given me I say to every one of you: Do not think of yourself more highly than you ought, but rather think of yourself with sober judgment, in accordance with the faith God has distributed to each of you. For just as each of us has one body with many members, and these members do not all have the same function, so in Christ we, though many, form one body, and each member belongs to

all the others. We have different gifts, according to the grace given to each of us. If your gift is prophesying, then prophesy in accordance with your faith; if it is serving, then serve; if it is teaching, then teach; if it is to encourage, then give encouragement; if it is giving, then give generously; if it is to lead, do it diligently; if it is to show mercy, do it cheerfully (Romans 12:3-8).

"Be merciful, just as your Father is merciful. Do not judge, and you will not be judged. Do not condemn, and you will not be condemned. Forgive, and you will be forgiven. Give, and it will be given to you. A good measure, pressed down, shaken together and running over, will be poured into your lap. For with the measure you use, it will be measured to you" (Luke 6:36-38).

And let us consider how we may spur one another on toward love and good deeds, not giving up meeting together, as some are in the habit of doing, but encouraging one another—and all the more as you see the Day approaching (Hebrews 10:24-25).

## 48

## Post-it Encouragements

*Leave a little Post-it love for your man.*

In my first book, *The Husband Project*, I made a list of thoughts you could write on a Post-it that would make your husband's day. That was one of the most popular chapters in the book. Then, we included it on my blog and also posted it to Pinterest. I get more hits on that list than almost any other pin on my boards.

So of course, I want to share it with you here for a little fun and simple encouragement you can share with your man.

## A Crib Sheet of 21 Post-it-Sized Encouragements

1. I'm praying for you today.
2. Those jeans are really working for you.
3. I love you.
4. You are the best dad.
5. You're the kind of husband that makes the other wives jealous.
6. You rock my world.
7. Can't wait to see you tonight—meet me upstairs…
8. Thanks for working hard to provide for us. I appreciate all that you do.
9. You make me feel beautiful.
10. I thank God for you every day.
11. How did I get so lucky, being married to a guy like you?
12. You're great.
13. You make every day more fun.
14. Have a great day.
15. You're hot.
16. I feel so safe with you.
17. Smart and good looking—I've got the whole package in you.
18. You can be very distracting, you know.
19. Our kids are so blessed to have a dad like you.
20. That smile I wear—it's all because of you.
21. God has blessed me in big ways by letting me be your wife.

# 49

# Pray for His Parenting

*Pray for him to be the kind of parent he wants to be.*

Moms and dads are made to parent differently. I know that isn't a shocking statement, but sometimes it's easy to forget.

God gives us the balance in our marriages. One of us is the disciplinarian, and one of us is the grace giver. It's our job to take that tension and apply it to being the best parenting team possible. And part of being that team for me and my husband has been praying for both of our parenting.

In our family, I was more of the heavy, whereas Roger was more laid-back. I used to think that if we were good parents, we would agree on every decision. But I've come to understand that the back and forth, the compromise, and then praying until we could come to an agreement (most of the time) was good not only for our parenting, it was also good for our marriage.

Here are a few of my favorite verses to pray for our parenting:

> Fathers, do not exasperate your children; instead, bring them up in the training and instruction of the Lord (Ephesians 6:4).

> Only be careful, and watch yourselves closely so that you do not forget the things your eyes have seen or let them fade from your heart as long as you live. Teach them to your children and to their children after them (Deuteronomy 4:9).

> Teach them to your children, talking about them when you sit at home and when you walk along the road, when you lie down and when you get up (Deuteronomy 11:19).

Discipline your children, and they will give you peace;
they will bring you the delights you desire.
(Proverbs 29:17)

Fathers, do not embitter your children, or they will become
discouraged (Colossians 3:21).

A gentle answer turns away wrath,
but a harsh word stirs up anger.
(Proverbs 15:1)

Whoever is patient has great understanding,
but one who is quick-tempered displays folly.
(Proverbs 14:29)

And whatever you do, whether in word or deed, do it all
in the name of the Lord Jesus, giving thanks to God the
Father through him (Colossians 3:17).

Do not let any unwholesome talk come out of your mouths,
but only what is helpful for building others up according
to their needs, that it may benefit those who listen (Ephesians 4:29).

If it is possible, as far as it depends on you, live at peace with
everyone (Romans 12:18).

## 50

## Make Him a Movie Star

*Create a video with him as the star.*

You can create this video using pictures of him or of just you talking
about the top ten reasons he is (you pick) wonderful, a good father, a
great husband, your main man, the man of your dreams, love of your
life, and so on.

"Every man wants to feel he is a star to his wife. Imagine how wonderful he will feel when you send him this.

"Here are some ideas of how you can make him a star:

- *Use Animoto.com.* You simply upload a few pictures, write a few text screens, select the music, and publish. You can then post to YouTube, Facebook, or send via email.

- *Record using your phone.* Record yourself using your phone video and send it to him at work. Most guys would love to have this on their phone to play over and over. You could even make it a family affair and record the kids as well.

- *Use Movie Maker or iMovie.* These simple programs allow you to include video, pictures, music, and your voice. Using these programs gives you more flexibility in creating your movie, but the end result is your man feels like a star!

"All of these can be posted online or sent via email. Imagine his delight to watch it on the TV if you have a smart TV."—Robin O'Neal Smith

······························ **51** ·····························

## Taking Care of Yourself Emotionally

· · · · · · · · · · · · · · · · · · · · · · · · · · · · · · · · · · · · · · · · · · · · ·

*Make sure that your emotional health is a priority. This is good for you, for your husband, and for your marriage.*

There is nothing my husband hates to see more than my being out of sorts.

When we were first married, blending a family was putting a huge strain on our marriage. I loved Roger desperately, but the resentment of the kids, the pain of trying to blend this family, and the constant feelings of failure made me sad a lot more than I imagined most newlyweds felt.

So we went to counseling. But the even smarter decision? Roger encouraged me to go to counseling on my own. At first, it felt selfish.

It's expensive. It takes a lot of time. I should be happy. Yes, the kids were a challenge, but I was happily married to a great guy! Love conquers all, right? But I felt like I was slipping. It wasn't a matter of Roger not loving me enough. It was a matter of me not feeling like enough in any part of my life.

I resisted. Roger insisted. He could tell that I was hating life—and he hated to see that. So I went to counseling. And it helped.

And I started to hang out with some different people—those who were excited about marriage and not always putting their husbands down. And it helped.

And I started going for walks. And figured out I had a vitamin D deficiency that was making me tired all the time, and started to recover from that. And it helped.

All of these little things started to build my mental health in a positive way. And while the biggest benefit was to me (I was nice again! I liked people again!), it did have a spinoff effect on my husband.

I'm not saying get healthy for your husband, but I am saying, when you get mentally in a better place, it can't help but affect your man in the best way possible.

- *Get some help.* I'm so grateful for the help of a Christian counselor who was nonjudgmental but challenged me to get mentally healthy. One of the best decisions I've ever made for myself or my marriage.

- *Hang out with good people.* I had to limit some of the relationships in my life that were surface friendships—they were draining and didn't make me feel any better about who I was. I needed people who told the truth, but with love.

- *Get on the same side in your marriage.* When you start off with the assumption that you and your husband are on the same side when it comes to finances, kids, and, well, life, it saves a lot of mental anguish. If you are not coming from that perspective, please seek out help. We are strong believers in good counseling early and as often as it's needed. It will save you a lot of pain down the road.

# 52

## Protect His Dignity

*Protect your husband's dignity every day.*

More than anyone else in his life, you have the ability to keep your husband's dignity intact. Never let him be shamed in front of you—by anyone.

It was awkward, to say the least. My husband had forgotten the garlic salt, again. He'd gone back into the house twice to get it, but between manning the barbecue, entertaining guests for his son's birthday, and holding a conversation with his daughter about the new ride at Disney, Roger had gotten distracted, again.

Which wouldn't have been a big deal, except his ex-wife was there to see the whole thing.

"Can you believe how forgetful he is? I swear, if his head wasn't attached, he would leave it behind everywhere he went." She said this in my general direction but so that everyone could hear.

Now I had two choices at this moment. Join in the teasing or stand up for my man. And that decision wasn't as easy as it seemed on the surface. I'd been working really hard to make a new kind of relationship with my stepkids' mom, so my first instinct was to join in on the good-natured ribbing. And I might have, if it had been anyone but my husband.

And because it was my husband, I knew that I needed to shut it down. I didn't want to start a precedent of it being me against him—I always want to land on his side.

So I said to her, "Actually, I'm always impressed how he can keep track of everything that's going on. If he forgets an occasional detail, it's because he's managing so much all the time."

It may seem like a little thing, but to my husband it meant a lot.

Here are a few other ways to protect his dignity every day:

- *Only speak well of him in public.* It's easy (and expected) to bash your husband when you are with certain groups. It does take some backbone to go against the crowd of women who are making jokes about how incapable their husbands are. But when you speak well, you give other wives the permission that they just may be looking for to do the same for their man.

- *Shut down negative talk from your kids.* Fifteen-year-olds are precious, aren't they? OK, some are—and some think that you and your husband are idiots and express that notion freely. Don't let them. Stand firm with your husband, even if he does always forget what time the kids need to be at school. And make sure that all your kids know that you and your husband stand up for each other—no matter what.
- *Post well, post often.* Opinions are formed on social media. Make sure that your peeps know what yours is of your man.

# 53

## Know the Truth—It's Not Fair

*Show your husband love even when you don't feel like it.*

So many of us are waiting for our marriage to be fair. It never will be—and that's a good thing.

With my first book, *The Husband Project: 21 Days of Loving Your Man, on Purpose and with a Plan,* there was an outcry from women everywhere.

"Why do I have to be the one who is always trying? I'm sick of being the one who is always working on our marriage."

"Why do I have to do nice things for him when he never does anything nice for me? It's not fair."

I get it. It's hard in a relationship when you feel like you're the one who is always making an effort. I've had friendships like this (and a few parent/child relationships). But there are several reasons why you may have to be the one extending yourself during certain times:

- *You husband is hurting.* Maybe he is going through a difficult time with his extended family and he needs a little extra grace.
- *Your husband is feeling unsure about himself.* Maybe he is struggling with your kids—or with you. In those situations it may feel more natural to retreat, but it really is an opportunity to show more love and extend yourself.
- *Your husband is going through changes.* Work is not going according to plan. He has a new boss and is having to prove himself all over again.

And you may be in a place where you really need him to step up and be more for you. Maybe you are hurting, feeling unsure about yourself, and going through changes. And maybe, right now, it isn't fair.

First, let me tell you, I've been there. Next, hear this—your husband may be doing the best he can right now.

There are times in our marriage that we need to get what we normally would expect from our spouse from other places. Here is what I do during those times:

- *I turn to Scripture.* When I'm feeling alone in my marriage— even if it's just for a day—the best thing I can do is fill myself up with God's Word. I know it's easy to get in my own head and start a pity party about why my husband isn't doing what he's supposed to do. But there are times that I'm looking for my husband to fill needs that he's not designed to fill. I must turn to God in those circumstances and put my reliance squarely at his feet.
- *I turn to friends.* God bless my girlfriends. The ones who will listen to me ramble. The ones who will pray for me and love on me and remind me who I am and who loves me, especially when I'm not feeling particularly loved.
- *I get busy loving.* I double down on my husband. If he is in such a hard place that he's having a hard time showing love, it means he needs to see it even more.

# 54

# Support His Crazy Dreams

*Start dreaming with your husband.*

Is there something your husband has always wanted to do? Is there any way you can help make that dream a reality? Now is the time.

My husband is a Disney fan. (I would say freak, but that makes it sound like he dresses up as Pluto on the weekends. He's not that into it.) Before we got married and for a couple of years afterward, he would go up to four times a year.

We still go to Disneyland a lot, but Roger's dream was to take our family to Disney World. So beginning two years before one of his big birthdays (the kind that has a zero on the end), our family dreamed, planned, and saved, and when the time came, we took an eight-day trip to the land of Mickey.

Was this my dream? My idea of being punished is to leave me in the sun, all day, crowded by people. So no. This wasn't my dream.

But the kids got on board and saved for the trip (they had to pay for their own room). I got on board because this was important to Roger. And in the end, we all agreed that this was one of the best vacations we'd ever had—hands down.

What is your husband's crazy dream? I'm guessing it's not eight days in the Magic Kingdom, but I'm also guessing it's something that you wouldn't necessarily wish for yourself.

Go ahead and dream with him anyway. Get tangible. Put money aside. Buy the maps. Get the books. Show him in concrete ways that you want to dream with him.

Some ways to dream with your husband:

- *Ask him.* Do you know what his dream is? My husband was pretty vocal about his, but not all husbands are. Ask him if there's something that he's always wanted to do, and then see if there's a way you can support him in that dream.

- *Put some cash on the table.* In order to make my husband's Disney World dream come true, we had to cut back in other areas of our spending. We stopped eating out, I ironed his shirts instead of taking them to the cleaners (he insisted he could iron his shirts, but he would just end up going to work a wrinkled mess). Figure out some ways to squeeze your budget to start saving toward his dream.

- *Do your research.* The best part of the dream is all the dreaming that leads up to it. Read the books, do the Internet searches, research the airfares, and start to turn that dream into a plan.

## 55

## Be His Girlfriend All Over Again

*To make your man feel special again, find some of that energy you put into him before you got married.*

"When we were dating, one of my favorite things to do was drive by Eric's apartment and leave little goodies on his doorstep, like a bag of Gummi Bears with an 'I'm thinking of you' note. Eric loved feeling special, and I loved being the one who could make him feel special.

"Now that we're married, I still like to leave little surprises for him just to let him know he's special. But I've applied the Gummi Bear Way to other things beside sweets and candy. As life has gotten busy with the treadmill aspects of parenting little kids, I've found that one area that frustrated me—date nights—has become my Gummi Bear Way of loving my husband.

"I used to think it didn't count if I had to set up a date night. Isn't the guy supposed to ask me out? It was always so frustrating—waiting, hinting, acting all bummed-out to try to get Eric's attention. I was really saying, 'I need some loving. I want romance. Don't you like me anymore?' But I'd try to get this message across to Eric by putting my unspoken expectations on him.

"Eventually, all those words would spill out in a puddle of tears. And those conversations would leave Eric feeling like I didn't appreciate all the other wonderful ways he loved me and took care of me—like waking up to feed the kids breakfast so I could sleep in or making sure my laptop was charged up by plugging it in at night.

"I didn't like how my conversations with Eric about date nights were changing the chemistry between us. He wasn't feeling special and I wasn't the one who could make him feel special.

"As I noodled over solving this date night conundrum, I had a flashback of myself standing in front of tubs of candy at the Sweet Factory, happily putting together a surprise for him, driving all the way across town, anticipating how happy he would be eating it and thinking of me.

"I realized God was saying, *Parenting right now is taking a lot out of your sweet hubby. Why don't you bring some sweetness into his life and arrange date nights with him just like you used to spend all that time and energy giving him a Gummi Bear surprise?*

"I realized in our current season of life, I can love Eric by giving us space to step away from the grind of parenthood and just be sweethearts. I found when I gave myself freedom to be his sweetheart this way, we both could step inside that soulful place inside each of us where I was his beloved and he was mine. I got the romance I really wanted by loving my husband the Gummi Bear Way."—Bonnie Gray

Here are a few additional thoughts on simple ways to make your husband feel special again:

- *Arrange the date.* Don't sit around being bitter that your man isn't courting you. Plan the date yourself (at least you are guaranteed to go somewhere that you like).

- *Arrange a sweet treat.* Like Bonnie and the Gummi Bears, figure out a way to delight your husband.

- *Arrange a note.* Let your man know you would date him all over again. Send him a note (you could even mail it to his office) just letting him know that he is still your favorite guy.

# 56

## Give Him Some Comfort from Home

*Stuff something familiar and comfortable
in his suitcase when he has to travel.*

The next time your man has to be away, give him something from
home that will remind him of you—and that you love him.

Here are some ideas of how to send some hometown love with
your man:

- *Jazz up his hotel coffee.* Hotel coffee is the worst. When Roger
  and I travel together, we usually buy some creamer so we don't
  have to use those awful powder packets—or worse, drink it
  black. But when he travels alone, I order some little packets of
  peppermint creamer, stuff a few in a Ziploc bag, and put them
  in his toiletries bag with a note.

- *Send him a whiff of something familiar.* I know it's totally corny,
  but I love the scent of Roger's shampoo on the sheets where
  I'm sleeping. So when he travels, I throw a pillowcase with a
  spritz of my favorite pillow spray and a note that tells him to
  slip it onto his pillow and have sweet dreams.

- *Upload your songs onto his iTunes.* Choose a few of your favorite
  songs and upload them onto his iTunes. Send him a note that
  you updated his playlist with some comforts of home.

# Load Him Up

*Load up his tablet with things he loves.*

We are cable cutters. This means that we have cut all cable access in our home. I don't know if we'll always live without cable, but for now, it's the right decision. We are trying to save money and to limit the amount of TV we watch. A word of caution: If your husband is a sports fanatic, I don't suggest cable cutting unless you want to see some severe withdrawal symptoms.

Yes, we still have Netflix and Hulu, so we aren't totally without TV, but it does mean that my hubby is making some huge sacrifices. And one of them is the Syfy network. My husband is missing getting his geek on.

So one of the ways that I can show him I love him is by loading up his tablet (or our Amazon Prime account) with the shows he loves.

Since we spend so much time traveling, and many airlines are still trying to get the whole inflight Wi-Fi figured out, it's good to get on the airplane with your tablet loaded up.

Surprise him the next time he goes to watch *The Big Bang Theory* reruns on his iPad. Stock him up with some fresh entertainment.

- *Buy the series.* I'm amazed at how cheaply a series can be purchased. Instead of cable, where you are paying for hundreds of hours that you don't watch, you can pay twenty-five dollars for ten hours that you will watch (over and over again).

- *Buy the movies.* If there was a flick you wanted to see but you never made it to the theater, or one your husband loved so much that you know he'd love to see it again, load it up.

- *Buy the audiobooks.* If your husband exercises or commutes, audiobooks can be a great solution for him. Load one into his phone and see if he likes that form of "reading."

# The Grand Gesture

*Do something wild, unexpected, and
over-the-top for your man.*

There are many advantages to living in California—the beach, the mountains, the weather. I am so spoiled by living here that my temperature comfort zone varies by about four degrees from seventy. But one of the distinct disadvantages, as far as my husband is concerned, is the lack of Dunkin' Donuts. Roger loves one particular donut there—the vanilla crème. He doesn't need anything else from Dunkin'. If they could just regularly ship a half dozen of those to our house, that would make my husband a very happy man.

So when I travel and I come across a Dunkin' Donuts, I make the grand gesture. I get a half dozen of the vanilla crème in a box. I then figure out a way to pack them in my carry-on. This works only on the day of the flight. Stale donuts are worse than no donuts at all.

Is it a pain? Yes. Do I get weird looks from security when I have to put them through the X-ray machine? Sometimes. Is it worth it? Always.

I'm guessing that your husband's craving may be a little more involved than six donuts. But there are other ways you can do the unexpected to make his day:

- *Hometown treat.* Is there something he grew up on—a burnt almond cake from his hometown bakery, a particular brand of sourdough that he loved growing up near San Francisco? See if you can get it shipped into town for a special occasion.
- *People.* Maybe it's not the food but the people he needs. Flying your daughter home for his birthday, buying tickets for him and his best friend to go to "The Game" (whatever game that is). An over-the-top gesture involving his people? Priceless.
- *Special events.* Waiting is the hardest part. One friend waited in

line to get her husband tickets to a concert that he'd been dying to go to. She was in line overnight and got the tickets (and left him completely in the dark until the night of the show).

## 59

## Keep Him in Stock

*Keep a stockpile of his favorite products.*

I wouldn't call my husband picky. He just knows what he likes.

I remember when we first got married, and I was shopping for essentials: toothpaste, deodorant, peanut butter. And I got it all wrong. I got the wrong toothpaste: "I like spearmint, not peppermint." I got the wrong deodorant: "I need the one with deodorant and antiperspirant." (I had no idea there was a difference.) I got the wrong peanut butter: "Chunky? Hmmm. I don't really like peanuts in my peanut butter." (I didn't point out the flaw in his logic. I was a newlywed and still trying to be nice.)

There really is an adjustment time after marriage. But we have had over a decade of adjusting time, and I'd like to think I know my husband pretty well. On paper, that is.

I'm not great at remembering all the little idiosyncrasies my quirky husband brings to the table, so I have them written down. Yep—I write them down and then I stock them up.

I buy his deodorant/antiperspirant a few at a time so we don't run out before the next time I'm at the right store. I buy his chunk-free peanut butter in bulk at Costco so we always have a supply. Every Christmas I buy him a pack of his favorite InkJoy pens so he is never without.

It may seem like a little thing, but it's a little thing that makes him feel taken care of and loved.

- *A weekly list.* There are a few fresh items my hubby loves to have on hand every week—a fresh cucumber for his salad, a couple of tomatoes for his sandwiches, and green bell pepper for everything. I have a weekly shopping list that I print off my computer that has these items already on there.

- *Things that won't go bad.* While I don't stock up on the Greek yogurt that he loves (that goes on the weekly list), I do lay in supplies of the things he loves that won't go bad right away, such as energy bars, coffee, and peppermint flavoring.

- *"Only once a years."* Maybe it's the McRib, peppermint ice cream (you know, the "limited edition" version with real chunks of peppermint in it), or Pecan Pie Pringles (yuck), but whatever your man loves, take advantage of the offer while it's still around.

## 60

## Learning to Listen

*Become an active listener in your husband's life.*

"People who know me know I'm a talker. It's hereditary. Many of my close friends are introverts, and they let me do all the talking when we're together. Not that I necessarily want to. They ask me questions about my life, I yammer on, go home, and then feel like a heel that I came away without knowing as much about them as they do about me. So I joined a mentoring program at church where I could learn how to listen.

"Then we had a crisis in our family, and I found myself suddenly the sole breadwinner and the caretaker of my husband as he recovered from a major illness. All of a sudden, we were together 24/7, and he needed a lot of support. I felt my working and taking care of the household while he healed was my way of affirming him, but it turns out I was wrong. It turns out that the listening skills I learned in the mentoring program were what made my husband feel loved and understood when he needed it the most.

"Of all the ways a wife can love and affirm her husband, who would have thought that the simple act of listening could make such a difference?"—Sherri Wilson Johnson

Here are some ideas for how to become a better listener:

- *Ask open-ended questions.* Questions that require only yes and no answers limit conversation and follow-up. Ask open-ended questions to find out more about your husband's day.
- *Do a two-day follow-up.* Say that on Monday night your husband told you about an issue that is going on at work. Put a note on your calendar to follow up with him on Wednesday. He'll love that you cared enough to ask.
- *Don't fix. Just listen.*

## 61

## Be That Milk and Cookies Mama

*Prepare an afternoon snack just like your mom used to do when you got home from school.*

Whip up a special treat for him and serve it to him when he gets home. Then sit and chat about the day as you enjoy the treat together.

Here are some ideas for how to get him snacking:

- *Go old school.* I think most of us remember a day when we walked into the house after school and smelled homemade cookies baking in the oven. And we all probably dropped our things right where we were and raced to the kitchen to grab a warm, gooey plateful. Do the same thing for your man. Time it so a warm batch of cookies is coming out of the oven just as he walks in the door. Invite him to sit down and serve him a few with a huge glass of cold milk.

- *Pick up something extra special.* There is this place in town that makes the best green smoothie in the world. (And if it has kale and spinach in it, then it has to be pretty darn delicious to get that label from me.) So a few weeks ago when I knew Roger wasn't feeling great, I picked one up for him and handed it to him while he worked. Let's just say he was in a much better mood when he finished. (And don't even start to tell me his mood change was because of the antioxidants in the kale. It was because of the love.)

- *Try something exotic.* A few weeks ago, one of my blogger friends from the South was raving about her new recipe for dill pimento cheese. I confess that my first thought was, *What in the world is dill pimento cheese? It sounds like a crazy Southerner thing that we would never eat in California.* But I went out on a limb and whipped up a batch, and you guys—I will never make fun of Southern cuisine again. And let's just say Roger was a fan.

# 62

## Be Alert

*Get alerts for the things your husband loves.*

This is a simple little tip, but if you do it, you will win major wife points.

I am on some pretty weird email lists. I get Amazon notifications about sci-fi author Terry Brooks, event updates from Disneyland, and weather updates about the best times to go stargazing in the Sierra Nevada Mountains.

I am not a fan of any of these things (at least not enough to sign up on an email list about them). But I'm a huge fan of my husband, and he's a huge fan of Terry Brooks, Disney, and astronomy. So I became a fan of the things he is a fan of.

I can give Roger a heads-up about the new ride at Disneyland. I can preorder the latest Brooks novel. I can clear our calendars so that Roger can go starwatching with his son, Jeremy.

I may not be interested in everything he's interested in, and that's OK. But I can be informed about the things he's interested in, and that makes me a better wife.

Here are just a few ways to keep his interest on your radar:

- *Sign up for Amazon alerts.* I love Amazon alerts—they let me know when Roger's favorite authors are coming out with a new book. I can preorder it for him, and it will often get here even before he knows a new book was coming out.

- *Check his cart.* We share an Amazon account, and often Roger will put things in his cart and forget to go back and buy them.

- *Get on the list.* Sign up for email alerts from his favorite stores. You will know when they are having a sale, and maybe even score a coupon or two.

## 63

## Super Simple Scripts 5

*Let your husband know how much being around him teaches you.*

"I learn so much from you."

My husband is smart. Like genius smart. (He would disagree. It would be the one time he is wrong.) My husband knows something about everything. And everything about some things. He has never tried to teach me to do what he does at work, but I learn something from him every single day. (Trust me, no one wants me coding their software for them. Or leading the teams that do.)

He shows me how to take a step back and look at every side of an argument, even though that goes against everything in my nature. (I'm more of a yell now, apologize later kinda girl.)

He teaches me to show grace to the kids (mixed in with my own brand of justice).

He models how to have patience with people who are trampling all over mine.

He demonstrates how to love people when they are not being lovable (especially when that person is me).

He serves without thinking about himself.

And I learn these things from him every single day. But it's not enough that I learn from him—it's important that I let him know that he is a role model to me in so many areas.

There are so many days that our husbands may feel like they're getting it all wrong. Those are the days that we especially need to let them know that we see plenty of right going on, and in fact, are learning from them every single day. (Even on the days that they're not feeling it.)

## 64

## A Verse to Pray for His Relationship with You

*Pray that you and your husband would be of one spirit and of one mind.*

This is a verse I like to pray for both my husband and me:

> Therefore if you have any encouragement from being united with Christ, if any comfort from his love, if any common sharing in the Spirit, if any tenderness and compassion, then make my joy complete by being like-minded, having the same love, being one in spirit and of one mind. Do nothing out of selfish ambition or vain conceit. Rather, in humility value others above yourselves, not looking to

your own interests but each of you to the interests of the others (Philippians 2:1-4).

My deepest desire in our marriage is that my husband and I would be of one spirit and of one mind—that we would serve each other in everything that we do. If we can get this one verse right, that really would be a marriage where joy would be complete.

"My prayer habit has made the biggest impact on my life, and as a consequence, on that of my wonderful husband, Bill. With the help of a wonderful friend and Christian mentor, I came up with some specific Scriptures listing blessings for my husband. I pray those aloud (and as close to daily as I can), in private, not where he can hear me.

"It has changed my heart, and now I look for those good qualities in my husband, whether he's actively showing them or not! I respond to him as a person who embodies those good qualities, and it has made me a much more pleasant wife and inspires in me lots of loving and spontaneous ways to show him my love and respect. God gets *all* my thanks for my husband, who is His wonderful blessing to my life."—Pamela Burr

## 65

## Ticket to Fun

*Buy or make him an evening of fun.*

"Everyone likes to have fun, but in the hectic day-to-day happenings of life, we often forget to plan for fun. This can be as expensive as tickets to a sporting event or a free homemade fun night at home.

"Building some fun into your mate's life will not only put a smile on his face and help him to release some stress, but will make you happy too.

"Here are some ideas of how you can give him a ticket to fun:

- *Buy him tickets to his favorite sporting event.* You can buy two tickets and go with him or let him invite a friend. Often my husband and son would go together to sporting events and that made both of them happy. Last year my husband invited a friend and they had a great time.

- *Tickets to movies or a play.* Not everyone is into sports. Perhaps he would enjoy movie tickets or a play or the opera. You know what your man likes and what would make him happy.

- *Make a ticket for a night of fun.* Let the kids help you make homemade tickets for a night of fun at home. Plan a board game night and invite friends. Serve his favorite snacks. Or if he isn't into board games, then maybe a 'watch the game on TV' night is in order.

- *You could turn this into a romantic evening.* Make a ticket on the computer to an evening of romance or games for just the two of you. You could give him a massage, play a board game, eat your favorite food, and just have fun together."—Robin O'Neal Smith

## 66
# He Needs to Know You're a Sure Thing

*Want to give your man more confidence in every area of his life? Make sure he knows he can succeed with the most important person in his life—you.*

"I want to take Carrie out for her birthday. Do you have any suggestions?" I was glad Mitch was asking my opinion. He and Carrie had been under a lot of stress lately, and their marriage was showing the signs. I loved that he was thinking ahead to her birthday next month.

"What about Napanthe? I know she loves the food there." I knew this would be a total winner of an idea. It was in Big Sur, about three hours from their house, but Big Sur is about the prettiest place on the planet. The perfect setting for a romantic dinner.

"Nah." Mitch sighed. "The last time I took her there she told me it was too far and a waste of gas."

"OK..." I said, pausing to think. "How about La Fondue?" This is the fancy place in town, big for graduations, proms, and San Jose Sharks' players.

"When I've suggested it before, she tells me it costs too much money."

"All right..." No wonder Mitch was a little frustrated. *I* was frustrated with Carrie. "How about a sure thing—the Cheesecake Factory?"

"Carrie says that's too many calories."

Sigh. So basically, Mitch would be in trouble if he didn't do anything for Carrie's birthday, but she had already let him know that every decision he'd made in the past was the wrong one.

So how do you not be that wife? The wife where nothing is ever good enough. The wife who picks apart every gesture so that your husband gets to the place where he thinks, *Why even try?*

Here are a few ways to give your husband confidence that he's doing a lot of things right:

- *Look for the good.* What is your husband awesome at? Roger opens the car door for me every time we get into the car. That would be easy to take for granted (and I did for way too long). But now I thank him every time. Plus, at least once a week, I make sure to point it out. "Thank you for getting my car door. You take such good care of me."

- *Brag on him.* Let others know, in front of him, what he does to love on you.

- *Get specific.* Some husbands just have no capacity for celebrating birthdays, Valentine's Day, anniversaries, or other special occasions. And for some guys, it feels like a big test that they are sure to fail anyway, so why bother? Why not have a real conversation (in advance of the event) about what would make it special? I've told my husband, "I want a card, a meal cooked for me (by you or the chef of your choice), and some sort of gift. Flowers from the supermarket are totally acceptable. Do those three things and you're golden." (For a man with an analytic personality like my guy, having a checklist is a gift.)

·········································· **67** ··········································

## I Feel Safe with You

*Let him know, in a variety of ways, that you feel safe with him.*

He locks the deadbolt at night.

He makes sure I have air in my tires.

He walks on the outside of the sidewalk so that (as he explains), "If a car comes up on the curb, I'll get the brunt of it."

He always helps me go through my checklist on the way to the airport: Driver's license? Check! Phone? Check! Debit card? Check! (His theory is that anything else I may have forgotten can be replaced. But those three things? Not so much.)

He's jumped in front of me when he thought a dog was coming after us (turns out it was a pit bull with an aggressive need for belly rubs), and he has me call him when I get to my hotel so that he knows I've arrived safely.

All of those little things make me feel safe and cared for. And it's important that I let him know that. It's important to him that he's "doing his job" when it comes to protecting me and the rest of our family. Even with our grownup girls, he will ditch work and hop in his car to take care of a flat tire. Just because they are his girls.

But like his need to know that he can provide for you, he needs to know he can protect you—and you are the only one who can let him know that he's doing his job.

Here are some ways to let him know that his protection makes you feel safe:

*101 Simple Ways* 129

- *Tell him why it's important.* "I sleep better at night knowing you are next to me."
- *Let him be your hero.* Yes, you can kill a spider, but you have a man around! Let him take care of the wildlife that gets into your house.
- *Tell your kids.* Let them know that between God and Daddy, the house is covered.

## 68

## Top Ten Things to Say to Your Husband as He Walks Through the Door

*Love your husband with affirming words
when he comes home from work.*

I get it—you may be the one walking through the door at the end of a long day. That's OK, you can still love him up with these words.

1. I've missed you today.
2. The best part of my day is getting to see you again.
3. I've got dinner. You go and relax.
4. I'm going to take the kids outside for a few minutes.
5. I put dinner in the slow cooker this morning, so we're ready to eat.
6. I just haven't been able to get you off my mind today.
7. I want to get the kids fed and in the bath so we can have some alone time. Can you help?
8. Nope. No plans for tonight. I'm all yours.
9. What do you want to watch?
10. Thanks for working hard at your job and at home.

The overall feeling your husband needs to experience in his own home is that he's doing something right, and when he gets home, he has landed in a safe place. Here is how my friend, author and speaker Sue Heimer, learned what her husband needed at the end of a long day.

"My husband, Curt, had all the signs of overload. He is quiet by nature, but I noticed he seemed to dip even further into his reserved communication with me. His face was drawn with signs of fatigue and even the gait of his walk had slowed. He spent more time in his chair with the remote in one hand, mindlessly skimming through the channels.

"I was aware that he had recently lost two huge contracts to competitors. He had worked on these projects for months with nothing to show for his efforts. To lose not just one but two deals made him question his ability to get the job done.

"I wanted to help. My heart ached for him, and I sought to ease the stress that seemed to stem from the rejection he was experiencing at work. So I began to ask him a question every morning: 'How can I serve you today?' or 'What can I do to ease your stress today?'

"Each day I would roll over in bed, snuggle up to him, and pose this same question. And every day he would give me the same answer: 'There is nothing you can do.'

"Weeks went by, and I gently continued my sincere request, and he would always repeat the same answer. However, I could tell by the tone of his voice and tender response that he appreciated my willingness to help in any way I could.

"One evening we were eating dinner, and I was trying to discuss a situation with him. He seemed very distracted and clearly was not listening, and I grew frustrated and then angry. I hopped up from the table and started stacking the dishes. My body language left no doubt that I was upset. Curt followed me into the kitchen and asked what was wrong. I shared with him what was bothering me, and he apologized. But I wouldn't let it go and stomped out of the room. (I am all mature like that.)

"Several minutes later he came up to me and said, 'I have so much stress at work right now, I don't need you to be upset with me too.'

"And there, hidden in his plea, he told me how I could serve him. He needed to know that even though he was experiencing great disappointment in his work, questioning his ability to get the job done, he was at least a success on the home front.

"How could I serve him? What could I do to ease his stress? I could extend extra grace during this difficult time."

## 69

## Hang Out with Good Friends

*Make sure you surround yourself with people who are building up your marriage, not tearing it down.*

Whether it's hanging out with girlfriends on a Tuesday night or double-dating with another couple on the weekend, make sure that the people you are hanging out with are contributing to your marriage.

A lot of married people are not big believers in marriage. They may have believed in it at one time, but since they are so miserable in their marriage, they feel that everyone else should be miserable in theirs.

But there are plenty of people who are working every day to make their marriage better. Hang out with those people. Yes, you can still be friends with those who have struggling marriages, but make sure you hang around some people who are building you up as well. That way, you can help build into the lives of your friends who are struggling.

- *Have some go-to prayer friends.* These are women who will pray for your marriage—without judgement, without piling on about what your husband should be doing and that you have every right to be mad at him.
- *Have some go-to couples.* Double-dating is hard, but keep trying until you find a couple that you click with.
- *Have some go-to girls.* I have a group of friends who, while they may see some trouble in their marriage from time to time, are

all working hard to have the best marriage possible. These are the ones who are going to point you in the right direction— even when you don't feel like going there.

## 70

## Love Apart

*Love your man by encouraging him to do things that don't involve you.*

"I entered marriage with a bit of a misconception. OK, a *big* misconception. I thought marriage meant you spent all your time together. Blame it on Hollywood or teenage novels, but I imagined regular walks at sunset, two baseball season tickets, weekly dinners by candlelight. Even handholding trips to the grocery store. I knew that we'd drive to separate jobs each day, but otherwise? Life would consist predominantly of togetherness.

"It didn't take long after 'I do' for me to realize how unrealistic this was. While it's true we must invest quality time and effort into making a relationship work, a healthy marriage also involves individual interests, friendships, and time spent outside the marriage. Which is why last year I sent my husband on a one-week scuba diving and deepsea fishing trip with his cousin. And *without* me. And not long before he sent me on a four-day writing retreat with three of my closest girlfriends. Because the truth is the healthiest couples are those who know not only how to be in love together, but also how to be in love apart."— Michele Cushatt

Here are some ideas you can use to encourage your husband to get refreshed and restored without you. (But then, he can bring all that good lovin' home to you.)

- *His family.* A couple of years ago I had a packed speaking schedule, and my husband just knew he needed to go visit his family. We were doing backbends trying to figure out my schedule until I said, "Maybe this trip you just go on your own." Turned out it was the right decision for all involved.

- *His friends.* Encourage him to hang out with his friends, on his own.

- *His ministry.* It's great when you can do ministry together, but if you are called to two different kinds of ministries, go build an orphanage in Mexico while your honey chaperones the junior high group on their Disney trip.

## 71

### A Verse to Pray When He Is
### Overcome with Worry

*When your husband is overwhelmed with worry,*
*get specific in your prayer to lift his burden.*

"Overcome with worry." *Overcome* and *worry* have to be two of the most defeating words in the English language. They each make you feel helpless—like there is nothing that can be done about the situation.

That is why I love Ephesians 3:20-21 so much: "To him who is able to do immeasurably more than all we ask or imagine, according to his power that is at work within us, to him be glory in the church and in Christ Jesus throughout all generations, for ever and ever! Amen."

God is able to do so much more that we can even think of. We are not alone, we are not overpowered. God is at work within us. We are not limited by our own power.

# Give Him Something Adorable to Look At

*Give him a picture of his family that will cheer
him up on even the gloomiest day.*

Display a picture of your family in a way that will make him smile,
laugh, and remember a happy moment whenever he sees it.
Here are some ideas of how to give him some photo love:

- *Buy a digital frame.* For a techy guy who has a boring, black-
  and-white office, a digital frame can be an ever-changing
  reminder of the family he loves and how much they love him.
  Just remember to load it up with fresh pictures every couple of
  months.

- *Let your kids be crafty.* I get it that interior design à la five-year-
  old isn't necessarily the most popular decorating style, but I
  can almost guarantee that your husband won't object if he gets
  an adorable frame from your kids. Head to the craft store and
  buy a blank frame and some acrylic paints and let your kids go
  to town.

- *Get silly.* Flip your kids upside down, let them stick out their
  tongues and wiggle their fingers, and snap some photos.
  Frame the silliest one and give your husband something to
  laugh at on those days when work—and life—is anything but
  funny.

# Four Ways to Let Your Kids Know That Your Husband Is a Hero

*Make your husband a hero in your kids' minds.*

Not only does your husband want to be a hero in your eyes, he wants to be a hero in his kids' eyes as well. You will determine, to a large part, how your kids see their dad.

Here are some ways to make your husband a hero in their minds:

- *Make sure they know how hard he works.* Sometimes kids think that everything they have comes out of thin air. Our kids need to know that Mom and Dad work hard. Point that out to your kids when you are driving the car, living in the house, and eating the food that his (and your) job provides.

- *Talk about how strong he is.* Kids love to think that their dad is the strongest in the world. Point out his strength when there's a jar that needs opening or some yardwork that needs doing (but you are not allowed to use this little tactic to get your honey-do list done).

- *Talk about what he's done.* Several years ago, our neighboring townhouse was on fire. We all ran outside yelling "Fire!" and got out safely. But then I had this niggling feeling, "Is Jeremy inside?" (It was the first day of college classes for my stepson, and I didn't know his schedule yet.) As soon as I shared this concern with Roger, he ran back into our house and threw open Jeremy's door—and there he was, asleep on the bed. I remind our kids regularly that Roger would run into a burning building for any of us.

- *Buy him the mug.* Those #1 Dad mugs may seem silly, but they send a subtle message to our kids about who their dad is and how they should think about him.

# 74

## Let Him Help

*Let him know specifically how he can help.*

I am friends with some amazing, talented, funny, godly women. Really—I'm amazing at picking my friends. But among even the best of women I see a disturbing trend that is making me a little crazy: refusing help from our husbands.

Now you may be thinking, *I've never refused help from my husband on anything.* But here is the conversation I hear over and over again:

Him: "Baby, what's wrong?"

Her: "Nothing."

I don't know if there is any more frustrating statement for a man than "Nothing." Because it does one of two things:

1. Leaves him feeling helpless and shut out. You feel rotten and you can't share with the person you are planning to spend the rest of your life with.

2. Leaves him feeling like he's in trouble. Because he probably is. You feel like he should already know what's wrong, and if he really truly cared, he would know.

Both of these situations make it so that you both lose.

But here's the problem: men's brains work very differently from ours. So what may seem completely standing-right-in-front-of-you obvious has probably completely escaped your husband's notice.

Here are a few things you may want to consider the next time you're upset:

- *Your husband may have no idea what is going on.* And that's OK. It doesn't mean he loves you any less, it just means his brain picks up on signals differently than your brain does.

- *If he notices that something is wrong, don't make him guess.* Tell him what the issue is, whether it's with him or not. (And if the issue is with him, assume the best, ask questions, and look for understanding.)

- *Give him some practical ways to help.* Maybe it's not conflict. Maybe you are just having a rough week at work. Give him a practical way to help you through it. "Thanks for asking. Work is killing me this week. In fact, if you could pick up dinner so I don't have to cook tonight, that would be a huge help."

## 75

## When Technology and Love Languages Meet

*Make sure you are filling up his need for appreciation.*

"My husband's love language is words of affirmation, and as it often goes, that is *not* my love language at all. To me, actions speak louder than words. So how do I encourage him when his language does not come naturally to me?

"Without even realizing it, I found a happy combination of words and my love of using the phone to communicate. One day my husband made homemade chicken-and-rice soup because I have a specialized diet and wasn't feeling well. Sitting at home enjoying the soup, I decided to send him a text. It simply said, 'Mmmm, belly full of chicken soup.'

"His response, 'Thanks for being so appreciative of my cooking. It does a good job of making me want to cook more.'

"So now I make it a point to use my phone in ways that will affirm my husband."—Luna Leverett

Here are some more simple ways to use that phone to affirm your man:

- *A picture is worth a thousand words.* Snap pictures of the things he has done and send him a text of thanks. Did he spend time with the kids at the park? Did he mow the lawn? I snapped a picture of my husband pulling a tree out of our backyard and sent him the pic with "That's my studly man!"

- *Tell the world.* Since people who love words of affirmation get a special boost from hearing you brag about them to others, you could post your thankfulness on social media. It could be words of thankfulness or sharing a picture of a gift he got you.
- *Share what others say.* Did one of your kids say something sweet about your man? Did you hear someone else speaking well of him? Send him a message right then while you're thinking of him. It may just be the boost that gets him through the day.

## 76

## Spoil Your Husband, Not Your Kids

*Make sure that everyone knows the hierarchy of relationships in the house—you and your husband come before anyone and the kids.*

For years I bought Neapolitan ice cream. Some of the kids liked vanilla, some liked chocolate. The strawberry? That's usually what Roger and I ended up eating. (Strawberry ice cream is like the Nicholas Cage movie of ice creams. No one is truly a fan, but if there's nothing better around, you might as well.) It took me years to realize that it was ridiculous. So I started to buy the fudge ripple with peanut butter cups that I knew Roger loved.

"Ewww. What happened to the good ice cream?" one disgruntled kid asked.

"I bought it, and you kids plowed through it," I said. "But this ice cream is for your dad. You can ask him if you can have some, but it's his."

"But it's gross."

"Ice cream is a treat. Your dad's treat is fudge ripple with peanut butter cups. It's not all about you."

Maybe I don't get the mom of the year award. But I may still be in the running for wife of the week.

Other ways you can show your husband that he is the priority:

- Our sit-down dinner, whenever possible, was served around my husband's schedule, not the kids'. Yes, I was pretty much in the kitchen and could talk with our kiddos while they ate early to get to a practice or rehearsal, but I sat down to eat with my husband.

- When three people are trying to get my attention, and one of them is my husband, he wins.

- Realize that spoiling your husband will be seen as a treat. Spoiling your kids will be seen as setting a precedent. "But last week you let me pick out my cookie from the bakery." When you spoil your kids, make it as infrequent as possible. Give them space to appreciate the treat. When it comes to your husband, spoil often.

## 77

## Empty His Plate

*Surprise him by taking a task off his list.*

Roger is in charge of several chores at our house. He is the bug killer, light fixer, computer maintainer, bottom-line dog walker (that means if we are both crazy busy and we can't go together, he will do it). There are dozens of other little things he does around the house that fill up his evenings and weekends.

But sometimes the man just needs a night (or weekend) off. Especially when things are super stressful at work. When there are deadlines looming and challenges in front of him, having something taken off his plate not only lightens his load but also indicates that I am on his team.

Here are just a few simple ideas of things you could do. Your man may not always do these chores himself, but if you do them, it's a clear indication that you are looking out for him:

- Pack his lunch the night before work.
- Gas up his car.
- Take the trash out before he gets home.

## 78

## The Power of a Well-Placed "Thank You"

*When it comes to your man, it would be*
*hard to say thank you too much.*

I've always known that women need love and men need respect. But I'd always felt weird telling my husband, "I respect you because…" It just feels weird and unnatural.

The good news. "I respect you because…" is not what my man needs to hear. We need to replace that with "Thank you for…" And here's the proof. Author Shaunti Feldhahn shares the results of her research in a blog post titled "The Thank You Connection":

> Over the past few years in my research, I have come to realize that what "I love you" says to a woman, "thank you" says to a man…"Thank you for clipping the hedges even though you weren't feeling well today" and "thank you for being willing to pick up the kids when I got stuck in a meeting" and "thank you for working so hard to support the family." It's stuff that we think often and say rarely. And since a man's primary need is appreciation and respect, we need to get in the habit of saying it! (See more at www

.shaunti.com/2013/10/thank-you-connection/#sthash. lpT2uDoN.dpuf.)

So what does that mean for you? Here are some ways to say thank you to your man:

- *Be specific.* "Thank you for picking up dinner last night when I was running late after work." Being specific helps your husband know that you are paying attention.
- *Let him know how he has helped you have a better day.* "Thank you for cleaning out the construction materials from the garage. I can't even tell you how nice it was to be able to park in there today!"
- *Let him know often.* "I know I say this all the time, but thank you for being such a great dad to the kids. They will grow up knowing how loved they are in a large part because of you."

## 79

## A Handwritten Letter of Love

*Write a love letter to your husband.*

I'd never thought about writing a love letter to my husband. But after reading about my friend Robin Smith's experience, I plan on writing one for our next anniversary—and the one after that. She even gives us a guide in case the last letter we wrote was to our pen pal in Nicaragua in the sixth grade.

"Many women long to have a letter of love written to them but never think about writing to their husband. I wrote my husband a love letter and gave it to him the day before we were married. It brought him to tears. He read and reread the letter. He has kept it and reread it many times during our almost thirty-year marriage.

"Since then I have received from him a wonderful love letter every year on our anniversary. I have selfishly enjoyed getting them. They are my prized possessions. If my house were on fire and I could save only one thing besides my family, it would be my letters. They are a snapshot of our lives, of our love, of our history. When I am down, or when I am upset with my husband, I read one of these letters and I feel better about everything. They usually put tears in my eyes and a smile on my face.

"While I look forward to receiving them, I have not taken the time to write my husband another letter. It will soon be our thirtieth anniversary, and I will be writing a love letter to him. It costs nothing, just a little time to put our thoughts and feelings on paper.

"If you are not sure what to write in a love letter here are some tips:

1. Most important is that it is from your heart—not what you think he wants to hear, but from your heart.

2. It can be handwritten or typed. Handwritten seems more personal, but if you type, make sure you sign it in longhand.

3. Make sure you include a date.

4. Things to include:
   - Dear _____
   - I love you. I am writing this letter because I want you to know how much you mean to me.
   - I love you because...

5. Other ideas you could consider including. Use the ones you are comfortable with or come up with your own:
   - Our life together means so much to me because...
   - I love it when you or we do...
   - You make me happy when...
   - I know you are stressed about _____ and I'd like to help by...
   - Our life isn't perfect, but I would not want to spend it with anyone but you.

- I'm looking forward to our future because...
- I look forward to spending many more years with you. I hope we can...
- When you do _____ around the house, it makes me feel loved.
- You are a wonderful husband and a fantastic father. I love it when you _____ with our kids.
- Our children are so fortunate to have you as a father.
- You are a wonderful stepfather, and I appreciate how you _____ with the kids.
- I love how you care for (others, parents, pets, friends, relatives). You make a huge difference in their lives.
- In closing, I just want you to know how much I love you and how blessed I feel to be a part of your life.
- I will always (love, care, have your back, be on your side, treasure our time together).

6. Be sure to sign it."

## 80

## Predecided Priorities Lessen Your Stress

*Your wife role is the most important relationship you will build into. Decide that in advance and build a better marriage.*

"Who on earth is calling at 11:47 p.m.?"

"Daniel and I roll over, hoping it's just a wrong number. But we sit bolt upright as we hear the voice of David, Daniel's brother, announcing through the answering machine: 'Mom's had a heart attack.'

"In the morning, as Daniel prepares to drive home, I start an inner debate: *Should I go with him or stay here? I have so much work to...*I stop. I already know the answer. I don't need to waste time or energy weighing the pros and cons. I just need to call the pet sitter and pack.

"You see, several months prior, God tapped me on the shoulder and invited me to make *Wife* a primary role in 2015. Initially, I wrote *Marriage* on my list of goals. But the check in my spirit made it clear that I'd missed God's point. He didn't want me focusing on marriage. He wanted me to be intentional as a wife.

"At the time, I had no idea *why*. Or *how*. I just knew that I was to put *Wife* on project status. In the weeks following the late-night phone call, I quickly figured out *why*. And learned *how*.

"Thankfully, Mom is on the mend. Daniel and I have weathered a month of multiple ten-hour round-trip drives, lots of sleep deprivation, and decades-old family drama.

"In the past, this would have driven me over the edge. I used to believe that lots of choices meant greater happiness. The more options available, the better off I'd be. So, for too many years, I gave myself permission to constantly rearrange my priorities. I called it 'freedom' and 'flexibility.' Which made me—and those I love—miserable. I'd start over from square one with each decision. I'd lie awake nights, haggling with myself. And then, even after I made a choice, I'd worry that I'd made the wrong one.

"But none of that happened last month. I didn't fret over *What's the right thing to do?* I already knew. Predeciding my priorities kept me calm in crisis, giving me more freedom and greater flexibility than I've ever had.

"Here's a little reminder of where your wife role ranks:

- You are a wife before you are a daughter.
- You are a wife before you are a mother.
- You are a wife before your career or volunteering at church or your child's school."—Cheri Gregory

# Email Love

*Send him some pictures via email that will
make him realize that you love him. A lot.*

Fill his inbox with sweet (and maybe spicy) little reminders that you
are thinking about him.

Here are some ideas of how to send some e-love:

- *Send a picture every hour.* Set a reminder on your phone to
  send your husband a selfie every hour of the day to remind
  him that you are thinking about him. The first one could be a
  picture of you puckering up, a later one could be of you cooking dinner, and the last one...well, we'll let you get creative
  with that one.

- *Remember him.* When you're out and about and you see something that reminds you of him, snap a picture and send it.
  There's this little Thai place where Roger and I had the best
  date night awhile back, so when I drove past the restaurant last
  week, I snapped a picture and sent it to him with the message,
  "Mmmmm. Pad Thai. Let's go again soon?"

- *Get all Pinteresty.* Everyone says that guys don't like Pinterest, but everyone is wrong. Because Roger loves Pinterest, at
  least when it gives me ideas on things to cook, make, or wear.
  Whenever I see a recipe for an amazing cookie or a delicious
  grilled dinner, or when I come across an adorable little outfit
  on Pinterest, I send it to Roger with a little note. "Shall I make
  these for you today?" He loves it. Even more when I follow
  through and actually make the thing.

# Gentleman's Choice

*Make note of his preferences, big and
small, when it comes to how you look.*

For your husband, it may be when you wear the blue shirt that makes
your eyes sparkle. Or maybe it's that perfume you wore when you were
first dating.

For my husband, it's my orange Mickey Mouse T-shirt. Yep—my
husband always gives me a compliment when I wear my orange T-shirt
from the Promised Land. (I promise that it's sweet, not weird.)

Do you know what your husband loves to see you in? I encourage you to notice if and when he lets you know what he likes you in. It
may be a compliment, a tap on the rear, or just a little extra attention.
Here are some ways you can highlight the things he loves.

- *Wear the jewelry he's given you.* Recently, I unearthed a necklace that my husband gave me our first year of marriage. It had
  probably been buried in my drawer for four years. Later in the
  day, when I was taking it off to get ready for bed, Roger said,
  "Thanks for wearing the necklace I gave you."

- *Wear the scent he likes.* Maybe not every day, but on the days
  that you will be spending a lot of time together, wear what he
  likes to smell. (And to make it last extra-long, layer it with the
  same scented bath gel and even the body lotion that you've
  never used from the gift set.)

- *Wear his favorite color.* If your husband loves you in pink, wear
  it on a day that you're hanging out (even if you are a redhead).
  Be sure to mention that the color choice is just for him.

# Throw Him a Party

*Dads and husbands can often get overlooked.*
*Make sure you celebrate him regularly.*

I'm guessing you do something for birthdays and Father's Day, but are there other times you could be celebrating your man?

Earlier this year, my husband and I received an engraved invitation to celebrate a coworker's daughter's sixth grade graduation at a local country club. When I graduated from sixth grade, I'm pretty sure my parents took me and my brother to McDonald's to celebrate on the way home. They let me order anything I wanted off the kids' menu.

Now with so many obligatory celebrations in our life (prom proposals, baby gender reveals, engagement parties, "bark mitzvahs"), it's easy to get celebrated out and forget that our man needs to be celebrated as well.

If he gets a promotion, completes a certification, coaches the winning Little League team, or just completes a huge project at work, it is a chance to celebrate your man. It also helps him walk more confidently through the world.

And it's not just for him. It's good to let your kids see that this is what a great marriage looks like—where we are each other's cheering sections.

Other ways you can celebrate your man:

- Bake him a cake. Write on it "I'm so proud of you!"

- Take him out to dinner to celebrate the completion of something at work.

- Have your kids help you make a sign that says, "We're proud of you, Dad!"

# Clean Underwear Is a Great Way to Say "I Love You"

*Taking care of the big and little things in his life is a great way to say "I love you."*

Never underestimate the power of clean clothes. Having a well-stocked underwear drawer, a stress-free closet, and at least a couple of choices of shirts and pants is a beautiful way to start the morning. And the only thing that equals not having any coffee in the house is not having clean underwear in your drawer.

No, laundry isn't all up to you. But I've learned that it is much more important to me than it is to the rest of the family. Until there's a crisis.

I am married to the sweetest engineer in the world who is also the most brand loyal person on the planet. And I know this seems crazy, but I have a picture on my phone of the brand and style of underwear Roger likes. (Yes, I've had to explain that pic to a friend who was scrolling through pictures of our kids.) So if I see that his are getting a little tattered, I can make sure that I'm replacing them with the ones he likes the next time I'm at Kohl's. I do this with socks as well—there is nothing that will drive my man crazier than a bulging seam at the toe of his sock.

So here are a couple of tricks that have helped me:

- *Have one lingerie wash bag for colored socks, one for white socks.* My friend Cheri Gregory taught me this little trick. All the socks go into their designated laundry bag, and almost half the time, they all have matches when I'm folding them. (I consider this a small miracle.)

- *Have a backup.* I have a pair of my husband's boxer briefs stored in my drawer. That way, if he is ever down to his last pair of skivvies, I have an emergency pair (and a clear indication that laundry is on high-alert status). I have a couple pairs of socks as well.

- *Make sure you have a supply.* I wash socks and underwear only once a week, so I know I need to have at least a week's worth of both for everyone in our family.

····················································· **85** ·····················································

## Post and Praise

*Affirm your husband through posts on social media.*

"One way I choose to affirm my hunky man is through social media. I mean, c'mon! Why not? We love to showcase awesome meals when we go out, talk about the incredible (or horrible) movie we just saw, express the ten thousand reasons why my kid is way more accomplished than your kid...so it would be crazy to bypass this obvious platform for hubby honor.

"Now, I'm not suggesting that you post things that are sappy or so over-the-top that people want to gag, but I can assure you that your husband will be validated when you post your excitement for the date night you are about to go on or when you publicly admire the way he cares for your family. Easy-peasy stuff. Post and praise. He will love it."—Gwen Smith

Three great times to post:

- When he does something great.
- Just because you love him.
- When he is especially sweet with one of your kids.

# Pray God's Word over Him

*Pray a specific verse over your husband
every day for a week.*

Choose a Scripture and pray it over your husband's life every day this week. Then choose a different Scripture and start again next week. Here are some ideas for how to get praying:

- *Google "Bible verses about..."* On a week when Roger had a huge work project due and was feeling overwhelmed, I googled "Bible verses about feeling overwhelmed" and found a list of verses about that topic. I chose Psalm 37:39 and spent the entire week praying that he would find his strength in the Lord and that Jesus would be his stronghold.

- *Send Post-its.* I love a good Post-it note—especially when it contains prayer and encouragement. Pray a specific verse over your husband, and then leave a note telling him what you were praying with a reference to the verse.

- *Commit to prayer.* One of the best things you can do for your husband is commit to praying for him daily and specifically. So make a commitment right now to pray for your husband every day for a week—a month, a year!—and intentionally pray Scripture for his life.

# Secret Agent Wife

*Bless your guy on the sly.*

Earlier this year I took my husband's car through the car wash. We'd both been talking about how grungy our cars were, so I told him that I needed to take his car to a hair appointment because mine was running low on gas. I was so proud of myself and wanted to get home to show him his bright shiny car. When I got to the house, I asked my son where Roger was, and Justen said, "He took your car to the car wash."

And that, my friends, is how you know you married well.

There are a thousand little ways to bless your husband, but you can amp the impact by doing it in secret. I love these ideas from my friend and blogger Emily Nelson:

"Here are two things I did to show my husband, Gregg, that I was thinking of him: I kidnapped his car while he was at work and got it detailed. He was ecstatic! Another time I polished all his shoes so he didn't have to. They were all clean and shiny and ready to go for him."

So simple, but I'm guessing Gregg had to look at his car twice to see if it really was his. I'm now planning some secret missions of my own:

- Slipping into his wallet a gift card to his favorite "eat out at work" place (which he never goes to because it's too expensive) with the words "Let me treat you to lunch" written on a Post-it note.

- Getting his propane tanks for the barbecue filled up and ordering the firewood so that he can do his two favorite summer activities: barbecuing meat and sitting outside by the fire.

- Ironing a ton of his work shirts so they are ready for this week.

# One Framed Photo

*Find a great picture of the two of you and frame it for him.*

Do you have a picture of the two of you that you especially love? Posting it on Facebook is great, but take it a step further and get it framed—either for your man to have on his desk or for you to keep for yourself.

Roger and I were at a conference in Monterey, California, and I wanted to get a picture by the bay. My selfie skills are not what they should be, but I've learned a few little tricks:

- You want either full sun or no sun. Shadows are a selfie's worst enemy.

- Use the mirror feature on your camera.

- The person with the longest arms takes the selfie—that's the rule.

- Always shoot from above. This will flatter both of you and decrease the number of chins in the picture.

- Take lots of pictures. This isn't 1985 where it costs twelve dollars to develop a four-dollar roll of film. The only thing a selfie costs is your husband's patience.

Once you have a great picture, either print it at home or send it to someone like Target.com to get the size print you want. Find a beautiful frame and pull it all together.

Whether it's for his desk or yours, he'll know how important he is to you.

## Give Him a Nudge Nudge Wink Wink

*Send your husband a message that lets him know
that tonight you want to...well, you know.*

One of the best ways to make your man feel loved is to show him he's
*loved*. So send him a message that lets him know that you want him
tonight.

Here are some ideas to get nudging:

- *Put on your cutest panties and let him catch a glimpse.* Put those
cotton boy shorts back into your drawer and dig to the bottom to find your teeniest, tiniest, raciest pair. Put them on.
Then let your husband catch a glimpse of what you're wearing.
If he raises his eyebrows at you, just wink and give him a little
kiss and say, "See you tonight, baby."

- *Come up with a secret symbol.* My friend Kelly has a blue coffee cup. It's just a plain old blue cup, but she told her husband
early on that whenever she is drinking out of it, it's a secret
symbol that she wants to have sex with him ASAP. She drinks
out of it often—she usually hand washes it so it doesn't languish in the dishwasher—and whenever she does, her husband's eyes light up.

- *Lay out your best laid plans.* Do something to your bedroom
to make it clear to your husband that you want to get busy
tonight. Light a candle. Fold back your satin sheets. Turn the
lights down low. Put on some mood music. And then lead
him in there and show him how much you love him.

# Build Him Up

*Write down a list of all the good things he
does, and then give him a compliment about
each of these, one every day for thirty days.*

"Include on your list all the things that make you happy and appreciative—anything from being a good dad to cleaning the toilet. It might
take you a couple days, but try to find thirty things. Imagine how wonderful he will feel to get thirty compliments from the person he loves.

"Here are some ideas of how you can build him up:

- *A compliment a day.* You can simply state the compliment each
  day. Or put it on a Post-it note on the bathroom mirror that
  he will see when he brushes his teeth. You could send it to him
  in a text or email. Doesn't matter how it is delivered, it will
  make a big difference in his day.

- *List of compliments.* You can make the list and put it on a big
  poster. Hang it on the fridge or send it in a letter.

- *Make a video.* Tell him in a video about all the things he does
  that make you happy. Send it to him on his phone.

"*Bonus:* Compliment him in front of friends, coworkers, or relatives.
Telling him how wonderful he is in front of others makes it extra special."—Robin O'Neal Smith

## Know the Truth—It's Not Up to Him

*Know that making you happy is not up to your husband.*

Yes, I get it—I'm writing a whole book on ways to show your husband you love him. But I also know that it is not up to you to make sure that your husband is happy. And vice versa.

The movies have made it clear that if we are going to fall in love with a man, he better be everything to us: best friend, provider, confidant, lover, savior, supporter. That's a lot to put on a mere mortal. Yes, there is a lot I want from my husband, but it's not up to him to make me happy.

Roger and I are involved in a lot of aspects of each other's lives. We do the parenting thing well together. We do the business thing well together. We do the vacation thing well together. But if I want to watch a sappy girl movie, I better call one of my friends. If I want to discuss the best ways to put together a nonfiction chapter outline, I better call one of my friends. If I want to have a *Gilmore Girls* marathon, I better call my daughter.

He is not designed to be everything to me, all the time.

But many wives are disappointed in their husbands for that very reason. They believe their husband should meet all their needs—all the time. And when he doesn't, they silently (or sometimes not so silently) carry that resentment with them for their entire marriage, letting their husbands know that they aren't doing what they should be doing to make them happy.

And we must stop.

When we build our husband up with our words, we are calling out the best in him—and making sure that we recognize who God created him to be.

My friend and marriage author Sheila Wray Gregoire shares some practical (and biblical) ways to magnify the best in our men:

"Men need respect. I hear this all the time—and sometimes it grates on me. Don't I need respect too? Why do I always have to be the one to offer praise?

"In marriage, though, we can either maintain our right to be 'right,' or we can grow our marriage. We can't do both. So let's praise and encourage our husband.

"If that's hard, think about it this way: *Praising your husband means that you're agreeing with God.*

"So many of us have a hard time praising our men because we don't feel particularly positive about them. If we try to force ourselves to say positive things, aren't we distorting the truth? And if I'm going to be honest with my husband, I need to be honest about my feelings, don't I?

"Well, yes. And no. To be honest means that you tell *the truth*. But what is the truth? *The truth is not always how you feel.* Telling the truth means agreeing with God about something because Jesus is the Truth. So praising your husband is the same as telling the truth about the positive things that God is doing in his life. You may be angry that your husband is lazy around the house, but has God made him a good provider? You may feel that he doesn't share his emotions enough, but is he a natural leader? Is he decisive? Is he easy to respect? Call out those positive things that you see in him.

"Your husband is a man whom God loves and whom God is molding. And when you call out the things in your husband's life and character that are good, you are agreeing with God about him. Even in the depths of our disagreements, when we take a step back and say, 'This is what I admire about you,' we put the focus back on what God is doing. And that's how you build a great marriage!"

Here are a few ways to take those unrealistic expectations off our man:

- *Recognize what he does do for you.* There are so many roles that your husband is good at. Make sure that you not only tell him what you appreciate but also make a note of it for yourself. When you start to recognize all the ways that he is already supporting you, it will be easier to let go of the ways that are harder for him.

- *Get some of your needs met elsewhere.* If your husband is an introvert, and you have a need for loud conversation with a bunch of people, organize a girls' night out. If you love to run, but your husband is closer to the couch than the 5K, ask a friend to go running with you.

# 92

## Speak in a Way Your Husband Can Hear

*While it's tempting to talk things out, sometimes our best approach is to wait, pray, and then proceed.*

"My husband's workplace was thrown into turmoil when difficulties between teachers and administration escalated into a full-blown crisis. Weeks of accusations, rumors, and secret meetings left him and everyone else involved exhausted and demoralized. By the time things started settling down, several key faculty members had sought new jobs and were packing to leave.

"Daniel was dismayed. He hated to lose valued colleagues who had become such a vital part of not just his job but his personal life as well. My husband has a deep sense of justice. And with every new rumor that surfaced, he longed to set the record straight on behalf of those being maligned.

"As alumni weekend drew closer, he began to say, 'If anyone asks me what happened, I am going to lay it on the line. I don't care how it comes across. The truth must be told!'

"Each time, my stomach twisted into a knot. Although appearances are few and far between, the Gregory Temper is infamous for its intensity...and insensitivity.

"I began to fret. *He's going to open his mouth, and everything he's worked so hard for so long will go right down the drain. He'll lose his job and act like a martyr, like it was the only manly thing to do. We'll have to move, and all the work will fall on me.*

"I felt desperate to control the situation. But I knew from years of experience that the more I grasped for control, the more it would elude me. And I couldn't think of anything to say to Daniel. Minimizing his concerns would backfire, making him all the more determined to speak up.

"One morning, while cleaning up after breakfast, I launched into a spontaneous conversational prayer. *What's my real concern here, Lord? I'm worried about something even deeper than a job loss or an unexpected move. What is it?*

"Instantly, a single word came to me: *integrity.*

*"Yes—that's it! My husband's integrity is at stake. But he doesn't see it.*

"I began to talk calmly as if Daniel were right there listening to me. I said nothing about his job, nothing about moving. I simply articulated my observations and concerns, based on our quarter-of-a-century together, in a logical manner. As I wondered if I'd ever have the opportunity to actually say these words to Daniel, I sensed the go-ahead from God to type up a letter expressing those concerns and affirming my support of him, and I left it on Daniel's computer chair.

"That evening at dinner, as we bowed together and Daniel blessed the food, he ended with, 'And thank you for my incredibly wise wife.'

"That was all. But it was more than enough.

"Alumni weekend came and went without incident. And I'm still not sure which thrilled me more: that my husband heard my words or that for once in our marriage, I'd communicated my concerns in a way he was able to hear."—Cheri Gregory

## 93

## Know the Truth—Your Husband Often Feels Inadequate

*Be careful with the words you use toward your husband.*

There are very few areas of your husband's life where he feels like he's crushing it. And if there is an area where he does feel like he is all over it, that feeling probably won't last for very long. And when you're disappointed in him? That is probably the worst feeling of all.

"He wants to be her hero," says relationship expert John Gray. "When she is disappointed and unhappy over anything, he feels like a failure. Many women today don't realize how vulnerable men are and how much they need love too."

If we knew how often our husband walks around feeling like a failure, I think we would be much more careful every day with the words we use toward him.

If there is an issue to bring up, assume the best and then discuss. Be frustrated with the action, not the person. And frame everything in acceptance and love.

## 94

## Verses to Pray for Your Marriage

*Pray regularly for your marriage.*

There are a lot of aspects of my marriage I need to be praying for regularly. Here are some of my favorite verses to pray over our relationship.

Let your conversation be always full of grace, seasoned with salt, so that you may know how to answer everyone (Colossians 4:6).

What, then, shall we say in response to these things? If God is for us, who can be against us? (Romans 8:31).

> Trust in the LORD with all your heart
> and lean not on your own understanding;
> in all your ways submit to him,
> and he will make your paths straight.
> (Proverbs 3:5-6)

For our struggle is not against flesh and blood, but against the rulers, against the authorities, against the powers of this dark world and against the spiritual forces of evil in the heavenly realms (Ephesians 6:12).

> The LORD's curse is on the house of the wicked,
> but he blesses the home of the righteous.
> (Proverbs3:33)

## 95

## Enter His World

*Try to figure out a way to enter into an
activity your husband loves.*

"Before Steve and I were married, I read a book by Sheldon Vanauken titled *A Severe Mercy*. In the book the author talked about how he and his wife, Davey, shared common interests to strengthen their marriage:

> "Look," we said, "what is it that draws two people into closeness and love? Of course there's the mystery of physical attraction, but beyond that it's the things they share...If one of us likes anything, there must be something to like in it—and the other must find it. That way we shall create a thousand strands, great and small, that will link us together. Then we shall be so close that it would be

impossible—unthinkable—for either of us to suppose that we could ever recreate such closeness with anyone else" ([New York: Bantam Books, 1977], 27).

"That's what I wanted with Steve—a thousand strands twisted into something unbreakable. So when he showed me his baseball card collection, I tried to pay attention. I didn't know the difference between Babe Ruth and Jackie Robinson, but I listened as he showed me his treasured cards. Honestly, I don't understand the excitement he gets by putting those cards in books, rating them on their condition, and gathering with other collectors to compare their finds. But I do love to watch the excitement in his eyes when he discovers a rare find.

"And while I knew I was never going to start collecting baseball cards, I decided that I could enter his world on some level. One year, when his birthday rolled around, I researched and found a large baseball card show in Philadelphia. I booked him a flight, rented him a car, and reserved him a hotel room. He was so surprised! It was one of his best birthday presents ever, and I was wife of the year (at least in his eyes). All because I entered his world.

"Interestingly, the next summer the ministry where I served was in a very dry time financially. It looked like we were not going to be able to meet our commitments. Even though Steve was a regular donor, he decided he wanted to do something more to help us get out of the summer slump. So he auctioned one of his prized baseball cards and helped us meet our financial obligations. He entered my world."— Sharon Jaynes

## Capture the Memories

*Create a scrapbook of your life together so far.*

"Your scrapbook can be a few pages or a whole book. Include one event or many highlights of major events. Think weddings, births, family events, and vacations. Or the simple everyday moments you treasure.

"Looking at pictures and remembering the good times is a great way to remind your man of happy times together.

"Here are some ideas of how you can create a memory album:

- *Purchase a scrapbook and include pictures, memorabilia, etc.* Just write a brief note beside each picture so he knows why you think that memory is special. You can find nice scrapbooks at Walmart or the Dollar Store. If you want to invest in higher quality, most craft stores carry a full line of scrapbooks.

- *Consider digital scrapbooks.* You create them online and then they can be viewed online or printed in softcover or hardcover. Some companies that provide this are Snapfish.com and Shut terfly.com.

- *Put an album together on Facebook and share with him.* Or use a program that I use, Keepy.me, which is intended for parents but could be used to make a scrapbook for the two of you.

- *Make the front of your fridge a scrapbook.* Use magnets to put pictures of special memories on your fridge. He will be reminded of happy times together every time he opens the door.

- *Make a collage of pictures* and frame them to hang on the wall for everyone to see. These are great in a family room or an entryway."—Robin O'Neal Smith

# A Verse to Pray for Understanding God's Plan for His Life

*Pray that your husband would recognize
that God has a plan for his life.*

"But seek first his kingdom and his righteousness, and all these things will be given to you as well" (Matthew 6:33).

Most likely, your husband is going to question himself and his place in the world, his place in your family, and his place in his career. Some people call this a midlife crisis, and it usually happens somewhere in the late thirties to early fifties. No wife ever thinks it's going to happen to her man, until it does.

Instead of being surprised by this event, if we can prepare for it—and especially pray for it—we can have an amazing impact on how our man handles this time in his life. Here are a few ideas of things we should pray for:

- Pray that our husbands would recognize that God has a plan for their lives, and it's a good plan.

- Pray that our husbands understand their value in their work, in their communities, and especially in their families.

- Pray that our husbands would not be distracted by the ways the world says that a man is supposed to live, but that they would carve out a path that honors God and honors the man God created him to be.

# Make Sure He's in the Picture

*Make sure you have plenty of pictures of Dad
with every member of your family.*

In families, it usually comes down to one of the parents being the photographer. Oh sure, when I was a stay-at-home mom, I took pics of my kids. But for family events, Roger is the one with the real camera (and not just the one that came standard on his Droid phone) and knows how to use it.

The problem? He's usually the one behind the camera. So I'm making a concerted effort to make sure he's in the picture. And yes, it's important to make sure that he has pics with the kids, but I also want to make sure that he and I have some great pictures, just the two of us.

It's OK to have some pictures of just you and the kids, but let's make sure not to call those "family pictures." Family pictures include Dad too.

Here are a few times to make sure that Dad gets in the picture:

- At kid's activities.
- For each birthday.
- During each holiday.

# 99

## Just Ask

*Be bold and ask your husband what you are
doing right in your marriage to bless him.*

As I was preparing to write this book, I asked Roger if he could tell me some of the things I did to bless him. Here is what he had to say:

"I am blessed by my wife, Kathi, in so many ways, from the everyday ('Wow, you did the dishes and you prepared dinner because I was working late. Thanks!') to the more extravagant, like getting everyone in our extended family to give me Disney gift cards for a year so I could get my annual pass. I am blessed. But I suspect she knows about these blessings. After all, they have been carried out with intentionality and thought.

"I am also blessed in ways that she may not be aware of. I am challenged to move outside my comfort zone (I never thought I would visit a country like Nicaragua), and in doing so, God has given us both new perspectives. I am blessed when I experience tremendous grace as I come up short on an event that is important to her. For some reason those events can be challenging for me. I am blessed as we plan life together and I realize that we share dreams and hopes for the life we get to live in God's magnificent world. I am blessed as we work side-by-side to realize the dreams God has planted in our hearts. I am truly blessed by the helpmate God has provided to me."

If you want to be inspired to keep blessing your man, it's simpler than writing a book—just ask him. After reading that email from my man, I can see the things that have stuck out to him and how I can be a better wife to him in the future.

Just ask.

166  *101 Simple Ways to Show Your Husband You Love Him*

## Let Him Go to His Box

*Don't expect your man to think like a woman.*

"In Genesis 1:27 it is clear that God created us male and female; we are different all the way down to our DNA. One way that difference is revealed is in the way our minds are wired—men tend to compartmentalize and women tend to integrate.

"Bill and I illustrate this difference with the title of our book *Men Are Like Waffles—Women Are Like Spaghetti*. If you follow a noodle around a plate of spaghetti, you notice it touches pretty much every other noodle on the plate. In the same way, a woman's mind integrates. Everything in a woman's life touches everything else.

"Guys tend to see things more like the top of a waffle with its separate compartments or boxes. Each topic gets a different box in a man's mind. So he thinks of only one thing at a time. When he's at work, he's at work. When he's mowing the lawn, he's mowing the lawn. And when he's watching TV, he is *only* watching TV.

"When it comes to the way we each relieve stress, this is different too. We women talk our way through stress. When I am stressed out my mom knows it, my sisters know it, my friends know it, my prayer partner knows it, Bill knows it, the clerk at the grocery store knows it.

"When men are stressed, they like to go to their favorite boxes to rest and recharge. God kind of helped us girls out so we could recognize these recharger boxes—most of them are shaped like boxes. The TV screen, the Xbox, the garage, the computer, the football field, basketball court, tennis court, the pool table, the refrigerator—all shaped like boxes.

"The bed box, or sex box, is a favorite box for husbands to spend time in. The sex box is like the free square in the middle of the bingo card, and husbands can get to this box from every other square on their waffle. A wise wife will make note of the importance of "the bingo box," and several of her husband's other favorite recharger boxes, and make space in their lives together for her husband to spend some time each week recharging. He will be happier—and so will she!"—Pam Farrel

## Stick with the Original Emotion

*Want to stay brave and reduce the conflict*
*in your marriage? Learn to stay vulnerable*
*and stick with your original emotion.*

My friend Fawn Weaver, founder of the Happy Wives Club, shared this article on her blog recently. I have so many women ask how they can stop arguing with their husbands. I couldn't say it any better than Fawn did, so I asked if I could include her words in this book. I am so grateful she said yes. Here's a slightly shortened version of what she wrote:

"Several years ago, I came home for lunch in the middle of my work day and did something I'd never done before. I sat on the couch and turned on the television. On my television screen that day sat Rosie O'Donnell on the couch that made Oprah the 'queen of talk.' Attempting to make reparations to her image, Rosie talked about the huge fight between her and Barbara Walters, which resulted in O'Donnell leaving the Emmy-award-winning show *The View*.

"Oprah asked, 'Do you regret that moment?'

"'Yes, I do,' O'Donnell responded. She said she regretted using her words as weapons and how her out-of-control rage 'scared' Walters. 'For me, at that moment, if I had been braver, I would have just cried and said, "You really hurt my feelings."'

"Oprah clapped her hands and said, 'That is so interesting! That you would say, "If I had been braver, I would have just cried." Because oftentimes crying is perceived as the weak thing to do.'

"She then asked O'Donnell why crying would have been braver than yelling and saying hurtful words.

"'Because then you're vulnerable. Then the authentic feeling that I had, [which] was pain and hurt and rejection [would have come out].' Instead, as she told Oprah, she put on the same armor she'd chosen to protect her since she was a child. She shielded her vulnerability and masked her hurt feelings with anger.

"Consider the last time you were in an argument with your spouse. What was the exact thing that set you off? I'm talking about what you felt, not what you discussed. What was your original emotion in that moment? Was it hurt? Fear? Sadness? Disappointment? Insecurity? What portion of your underbelly was exposed?

"When we become angry enough to begin arguing, especially with someone we love as much as our spouse, we have allowed the original emotion—which would expose our vulnerability—to be covered up by a more aggressive, defensive response.

"Rather than exposing the softer side of ourselves, we put up a shield and pull out our verbal sword and begin swinging. We swing left, we swing right, aimlessly out of control and missing the target every time. Yes, we may slice and dice the heart of our spouse, but we miss the mark because we've not dealt with the true emotion we're feeling.

"There is one secret I have kept to myself for all these years. And if I hadn't accidentally let it slip in a recent interview, it would probably still be my little secret. Well, here goes...(Please don't judge.)

"My husband, Keith, and I—in our nearly eleven years of marriage—have *never* argued. Anyone who knows us can attest to us both being strong and independent people, but in all that time, I've never raised my voice at him and he's never raised his at me.

"We talk about everything. And I mean *everything*. We don't suppress or repress our feelings and we never say things under our breath. We don't sweep anything under the rug. If he does something I don't like, I let him know it. When I do something he's not very fond of, you better believe he lets me know. And yet, we've never argued. How is that even possible? The short answer is this: (1) Mutual respect, and (2) We stick to the original emotion.

"We strive, every moment we are together, to remain vulnerable with one another. Yes, that can feel strange at first, but I have to tell you, it feels amazing because we've never wasted time making up. Now, of course, that means we've never experienced 'makeup sex' (which I hear can be pretty fantastic). But then again, why not figure out a way to create that passion—inside and outside of the bed—without the preceding anger?

"Most of us are taught from an early age that arguing is normal. Getting mad is how couples communicate when upset. We are shown how to guard our true feelings and emotions by protecting our hearts. We learn that it's better to go on the offensive than to find ourselves exposed. The problem with all this in marriage is that learned behavior leads to blind conversations. You're never really fighting about what it is you think you are fighting about.

"*Sticking with the original emotion—remaining in a place of vulnerability—is the crux of bypassing arguments and getting to the heart of a matter.* My husband and I didn't learn our 'love languages' until we'd been married nine years. But it didn't matter because our respect for one another was so great that everything we did and said was with love and the highest amount of honor.

"Mutual vulnerability and respect allows you both to lay it all out on the table. Your dreams, hopes, ambitions, fears, hurt...nothing is off-limits.

"We can't keep everything bottled inside. We all need to have that one person we can be completely honest with about our perceived failures, hurts, successes, and hopes. We need to have at least one person who will love and respect us unconditionally. Who better than the one who shares your bed at night to share your deepest desires also?

"As Rosie O'Donnell reminded us all through her uncontrolled rage that fateful day in Barbara Walters' dressing room: there is great wisdom in sticking with the original emotion, if we would just be brave enough to be vulnerable."

Yes. One thousand times yes. Be brave. Be vulnerable. Stick with the original emotion. Here are a couple of ways to walk this out:

- *Don't mask with other emotions.* Some people see sadness or disappointment as weakness, so they move on to anger and frustration with their partner. Sit in the sadness for a while, and then bravely express it. Sadness keeps you from projecting your emotions onto your partner and lets you deal with the situation at hand.

- *Practice being brave.* In small ways, show up for your

emotions, don't push down or ignore them. If you have a pattern of going off on each other, try this in discussions about where to go out for dinner—not in discussions about your mother-in-law.

- *Check in with yourself.* What are you truly feeling? I know that when I'm hurting, there is a temporary release in lashing out at other people. (I didn't say it was pretty, I said it was true.) But that is a bad short-term fix to a problem that will only make it worse. Check in with yourself and see what you are feeling and then what you can do about it. Ask your partner for support. Grow together.

# About the Author

Dear Reader,

Thanks for being a part of *101 Simple Ways to Show Your Husband You Love Him*. One of the greatest privileges I have is to hear back from the people who have used my books. I would love to stay in touch.

**Website:** www.KathiLipp.com

**Facebook:** facebook.com/authorkathilipp

**Twitter:** twitter.com/kathilipp

**Mail:** Kathi Lipp
171 Branham Lane
Suite 10-122
San Jose, CA 95136

In his grace,

*Kathi Lipp*

## Happy Habits for Every Couple

*21 Days to a Better Relationship*

When was the last time you flirted with your husband? Was it before you had kids?

Do you spend more time on the couch with your wife watching movies or with a bag of chips watching The Game?

Does your idea of a hot date include a drive-thru and springing for the extra-large fries?

What would your marriage look like if for 21 days you turned your attention to happy habits that will better your relationship? Plenty of books describe how to improve a marriage, how to save a marriage, even how to ramp up intimacy in a marriage. In *Happy Habits for Every Couple*, Kathi Lipp and husband Roger show you practical, fun-filled ways to put love and laughter back into your marriage.

Here are just a few of the results you'll see when you put *Happy Habits for Every Couple* into practice:

- new levels of warmth and tenderness in your relationship

- a deeper sense of security with your spouse

- a marriage filled with fun and flirting

If you haven't given up the dream of being head-over-heels with your spouse again, following this 21-day plan will give you just the boost you need to bring you closer together.

## Clutter Free

If you've ever wished you could clear out your clutter, simplify your space, and take back your life, Kathi Lipp has just the solutions you need. Building off the success of her *The Get Yourself Organized Project*, this book will provide even more ideas for getting your life and your stuff under control.

Do any of these descriptions apply to you?

- You bought a box of cereal at the store, and then discovered you have several boxes at home that are already past the "best by" date.

- You bought a book and put it on your nightstand (right on top of ten others you've bought recently), but you have yet to open it.

- You keep hundreds of DVDs around even though you watch everything online now and aren't really sure where the remote for the DVD player is.

- You spend valuable time moving your piles around the house, but you can never find that piece of paper when you need it.

- Your house makes you depressed the moment you step into it.

As you try out the many easy, doable solutions that helped Kathi win her battle with clutter, you'll begin to understand why you hold on to the things you do, eliminate what's crowding out real life, and make room for the life of true abundance God wants for you.

To learn more about Harvest House books and
to read sample chapters, visit our website:

**www.harvesthousepublishers.com**